A GUIDE TO TRACING YOUR CORK ANCESTORS

A Guide to Tracing your Cork Ancestors

Tony McCarthy
and
Tim Cadogan

FLYLEAF PRESS

First published in 1998 by
Flyleaf Press
4 Spencer Villas
Glenageary
Co. Dublin
Ireland
flyleaf@indigo.ie

British Library cataloguing in Publication Data available

ISBN   0 9508466 8 6

Cover design by Cathy Henderson showing a scene from the
Coal Quay market in Cork City.

Printed and produced by e print Limited
email: books@eprint.ie

Dedication

To
Rev. W. Maziere Brady, DD,
Rev. Bartholomew O'Keeffe, DD,
Richard Henchion,
and
all others who helped to preserve
the genealogical records of Cork

'Sad havoc among the materials for such a work was occasioned by the disturbances of 1641 and 1688, and since then the ignorance and carelessness of their custodians caused the destruction or loss of many a Parish Register and Visitation Book, which the wars had spared. Nor is it easy always to search the Diocesan Registries. Inquirers, armed with the permission of the Bishop, may yet be baffled by surly officials, or disconcerted by the want of proper catalogues and indexes, or driven away by dust and dirt before the musty and ill-scented documents be fully examined'.

W. Maziere Brady, DD
Chaplain to the Lord Lieutenant
and Vicar of Clonfert, Cloyne
1863

Table of Contents

Abbreviations Used

To facilitate the reader, an effort has been made to keep abbreviations to the minimum. The abbreviations below in bold are used throughout because of the length of the titles and the frequency with these titles are cited.

IA: *Irish Ancestor,* Vols 1-18, 1969-1986

IG: *Irish Genealogist: official organ of the Irish Genealogical Research Society*, Vol. 1, No. 1, 1937-proceeding

IGP: The Irish Genealogical Project

JCHAS: *Journal of the Cork Historical and Archaeological Society*, Vol. 1A-3A, 1892-94; second series, Vol. 1, 1895-proceeding

O'Kief: *O'Kief Coshe Mang Slieve Lougher and Upper Blackwater in Ireland*, 15 Vols, Birmingham, Alabama: Casey, 1952-1971

TAB: Tithe Applotment Book

Tables and Illustrations

Chapter 1 Introduction

Tracing your Cork ancestors: within the confines of this small book, it is not possible to deal comprehensively with this theme. Some explanation, therefore, is required with regard to what we have left out and what we have focused on.

Cork is the biggest of Ireland's 32 counties. With an area of almost 3,000 square miles it constitutes roughly nine per cent of the island, and it has a population to match. The 1841 census indicated that 850,000 people, that is ten per cent of the entire population, lived in Cork. The most recent census showed the county to have over 420,000 inhabitants — retaining its overall proportion of Ireland's population today. The second city of the Republic, also called Cork, lies within the confines of the county, as do about twenty sizeable — by Irish standards at least — towns. Down-river from Cork is the harbour town of Cobh, formerly Queenstown and earlier called Cove or the Cove of Cork. This was the principal port of emigration from Ireland to North America from the late 1850s for almost a century. In size and population, Cork is three times as large as the average Irish county. The book makes an effort to range over the whole county.

As in the rest of Ireland, Cork people belonged to different social classes, different religious denominations, and worked at a variety of jobs. These factors are important as far as genealogical research is concerned, and none of the major groupings is ignored.

A very old tradition, recorded in the 'Annals of the Four Masters', states that the first people who came to Ireland, landed in Cork, and archaeologists have confirmed that the county has been inhabited for thousands of years. But even the most optimistic of genealogists does not expect his research to carry him back to remote times. For the majority of Irish people, genealogically relevant documentation runs out around the beginning of the nineteenth century. The book, therefore, concentrates on records generated over the last two centuries.

People researching Cork-based family trees can have quite different needs as far as advice is concerned. Some may be just getting used to the basics, while others may be deeply involved in arcane sources. It was thought best to presuppose very little knowledge on the part of the reader, so bear with us when we explain the obvious. The more advanced researcher, should find the tables of information on parish records useful, and may come across occasional references to some local sources which may not have come up for attention previously.

The regard that Cork people have for their city and county has often been commented upon. This loyalty towards their proud old mercantile city reminded one commentator of the city-state patriotism of Italian towns. In the time period being dealt with, neither Cork City nor county was independent of the rest of Ireland, they were simply a part of the much larger administrative unit — Ireland. For this reason there is a certain artificiality in writing about Cork as if it were an independent republic, and it should be remembered that much of what is said in the following pages about genealogical records applies also in large measure to the other 31 counties. However, country-wide records were not so uniform as to be without regional variations. So, the all-Ireland sources are dealt with, with an emphasis on Cork. Dealing exclusively with one county allows the scope to consider the local character of such records. Also, specifically local sources, such as Cork newspapers and Cork archives can be examined in some detail. This local bias should also be evident in other areas, such as the treatment of administrative divisions. The local focus makes it possible to include civil parish lists and maps, and lists of ecclesiastical parishes and their records.

Many books on Irish genealogy seem to assume that the reader will not be resident in Ireland. Unfortunately, up to recent times at least, that assumption would have been correct. However, we take a more hopeful view — that Irish people are at last taking as serious an interest in their roots as the descendants of Irish emigrants living in the wider Irish world. Therefore, we thought it appropriate to include advice on carrying out research in Cork. This, needless to say, is in addition to dealing with how to conduct research in the main archives in Dublin. Many genealogically relevant records are available in various Cork libraries and archives — a fact which makes it unnecessary for locals to be continuously travelling to Dublin. Even if you are not living in Cork, it might be more interesting to do some of the research work on your Cork ancestors in Cork.

The book has been laid out in the following manner. After this brief introduction, there is a chapter dealing with preliminaries. A methodical approach to the task of tracing your ancestors is suggested. This is followed by a chapter on Irish administrative divisions, a knowledge of which is essential for anyone contemplating Irish genealogical research. The chapters which follow describe in detail the various types of records in which information about Cork ancestors may be found, the locations of these records and the finding aids available for researching them. The final chapters take you on a tour of the Cork archives and libraries, and of the main Dublin repositories in which the records may be examined. Useful information such as addresses and opening times of archives, and suggestions for further reading have been consigned to the final chapter.

We hope that there will be something in the book for all those who have located an ancestor in Cork whom they wish to research.

Chapter 2   Preliminaries

If you chop the head off a chicken, some quirk of its nervous system permits it to run around for a while, to enjoy a few last moments of frenzied activity. The headless chicken is often used to symbolise the human being who is always busy but getting nowhere. The approach that many people have to the work of genealogy could be described as the headless chicken technique. Essentially it involves intense but undirected activity: rushing from one archive to another, jumping from one series of records to another, forming one theory after another.

If you clarify what you are attempting to do at the outset and spend a little time planning how you hope to achieve your goals, you can avoid this wasteful procedure. Before looking at any documents, you should find out from relatives as much information about your ancestors as possible. Elderly people are the greatest source of genealogical information. Parents, grandparents and great grandparents should all be consulted; uncles, aunts, cousins and even more distant relations may also have something to impart. Don't forget to collect copies of letters, photographs and other documents. Normally, such information is available free of charge and with little effort on the part of the researcher. In contrast, once you start archival research, genealogy becomes both difficult and expensive, particularly if you have to travel some distance to those sources.

It is important to record the information you gather. As more and more ancestors and other relations come into the picture, the necessity for some scheme for recording, storing and accessing information becomes clear. Genealogy is an old and popular pastime and many methods of coping with family history data have been established. Members of the Church of Jesus Christ of Latter-day Saints — also known as the Mormons — believe that their deceased ancestors may be baptised and become posthumous members of their Church. Mormons, therefore, have a very keen interest in genealogy. The Church, to facilitate this interest, has produced pedigree charts and family group charts which makes recording the basic details of individuals and families very easy. These charts also have another advantage in that they can be linked to one another by a system of letters and numbers. The charts have no special religious application and may be used by anyone. They are A4 size sheets and may be photocopied easily. The use of computer packages to record family history is also becoming very popular. There are many such packages of varying price and complexity.

Many people world-wide find the Sosa Stradonitz numeric system to be a very simple and effective way of keeping track of ancestral information. This scheme was invented in 1676 by De Sosa and then revised in 1898 by Von Stradonitz, both of these men being accomplished genealogists. With this method, the number 1 is allocated to the person whose family history is to be established; the same number also represents that individual's brothers and sisters. The number 2 is allocated to the father and the number 3 to the mother. Going back another generation, the paternal grandfather is given the number 4, the paternal grandmother, the number 5, the maternal grandfather is number 6 and the maternal grandmother is number 7 (illustration below). Thus, even numbers are always given to males and odd

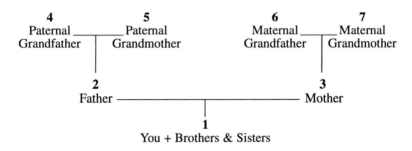

Sosa Stradoniz Numeric System

numbers to females; a father will always bear a number which is twice the value of that of his child; a mother will always bear a number which is twice the value of that of her child plus 1, or equal to the value of that of her husband plus 1. When individuals in a family tree are given numbers, it makes it much easier to file away information about them and to find it afterwards. The method you choose for recording and keeping track of your information does not matter. What does matter is that you have some method of doing so.

When you have exhausted the living sources of information, and you have recorded the data you collected up to that point, you must then turn to documents if you wish to make further progress. The 1901 census is usually the best starting point. This may seem too recent for many people, and for emigrants tracing Irish ancestors, it may not be suitable as their ancestors may have left Ireland before 1901. However, if the 1901 census falls within the time period which you are researching, it is unlikely that you will ever find more information about your ancestors on a single sheet than is to be found in the relevant 1901 census form. Such a form is like a snapshot of your ancestors as they were in 1901. The 1911 census should be examined next, followed by research in the registers of births, deaths and marriages. Griffith's _Valuation_ , the tithe applotment books and the relevant church registers should then be searched, in that order. After that, it depends very much on what you have found out. More advice on how to proceed will be given in the following chapters, each of which deals with a particular source.

The starting point of your family tree is yourself. The most frequently cited rule of genealogy is to go from the known to the unknown. The connection between yourself and your parents will be known to you and well documented. That between your parents and grandparents will be a little less well known and getting the documentation, like birth and marriage certificates, may be a bit more troublesome. As you follow the chain back farther, the journey becomes more and more difficult. But you must resist at all times the temptation to make assumptions, jump generations, or to graft yourself onto an existing pedigree with the aid of scant evidence and wishful thinking. Genealogy is a branch of history and requires the same scholarly approach. Some genealogists seek three documentary proofs before they accept a parent-child connection as valid.

There is a time to finish, a time to make something out of all the information you have collected. To give your work a chance of surviving, it must be rendered into some interesting form. The simplest is a pedigree chart with, perhaps, some additional information written in. A manuscript with the addition of photographs could be considered. If a more elaborate scheme is contemplated, some thought should be given to mentioning the sources of your information. A family history must be accurate, otherwise it is not worth doing; it must be entertaining otherwise it will not be read by anyone. You may intend to get a personal computer, to get the appropriate software, to get lessons on how to use them, to type in all your data and to produce the perfect family history. In the short-term, however, it might be an idea to follow the age-old tradition of writing some basic family details into the family Bible.

There are those, of course, who never finish, who spend their time following leads and postponing the onerous task of writing up the family history. After the amateur genealogist has, perhaps, gone on to actually meet those ancestors who have so tantalisingly eluded him during the whole course of his lifetime, what happens to his research materials? What happens to all of those certificates, those newspaper cuttings, photocopies, old photographs and other treasures that took years to compile? The unpalatable but obvious truth of the matter is that your life's work, having all the outer appearances of rubbish, is thrown out.

154   VIVACITY OF THE PEOPLE.

people. Here, as elsewhere, their countenances and general conduct indicated the greatest vivacity, cheerfulness, and good humour. The town belongs to the Earl of Kingston, whose castle, of which we caught a glimpse through the trees that surround it, seemed to be a splendid building. It was erected in 1823. The grounds are very beautiful, and the public are liberally allowed free access.

The labourers here, when employed, have sixpence per day and diet. The single men go to Mitchellstown on a Sunday to hire for the week, and get 1s. 6d. or 2s. and diet, per week. For a house and garden they pay from thirty to five-and-thirty shillings; for conacre-ground, £5 per acre. The ready-money price of potatoes is 3d., the credit price 5d. per stone; the price of pork is 2¾d. per lb.

Page from "The Miseries and Beauties of Ireland" by Jonathan Binns, London 1837, on the people of Mitchellstown

Chapter 3   Emigration & Emigration Sources

For the overseas family researcher whose County Cork ancestor was an emigrant, a knowledge of emigration history and patterns from Ireland to the country or region of interest will be useful both as an aid to research and as part of the family history. There is now a substantial literature in the field of emigration studies, much of it based on primary sources, which in turn can benefit the genealogist. Even if documentary evidence of the details of an ancestor's emigration proves elusive, an accurate picture of emigration patterns at the time will be a valuable guide to the family historian's further research.

It is ironic that emigration records, the genealogical source least likely to be located in Ireland, are among those most frequently sought by overseas visitors, especially those from the US. Unfortunately, there are, in practical terms, scarcely any original passenger lists in Irish archives nor any 'registers' of Irish emigrants. No official records of emigrants were created at the port of departure and such records as shipping companies may have created have disappeared in almost all cases. The search for surviving records of emigration is more likely to be fruitful in the country of destination, especially in the US and Australia. It may be worth noting here that passage between Great Britain and Ireland involved no documentation and consequently there are no records of Irish emigrants or migratory labourers to Britain.

Obviously, establishing when an ancestor arrived in the adoptive country is a key element in any researcher's schedule, but, otherwise, passenger lists do not provide a great deal of genealogical data as they rarely identify place of origin of the emigrant. Prior to the establishment of Queenstown (Cobh) as a trans-Atlantic port of call, c.1859, most County Cork (and Irish) emigrants departed from Liverpool, negating even the value of knowing the port of departure. (In 1846-51, the port of Cork provided only 2.1 per cent of Irish emigrants arriving in the port of New York). While a larger proportion of Irish emigration to Canada, an important emigrant destination up to the late 1840s, was conducted from Irish ports, including several in County Cork, Canadian passenger records for the relevant period are not extant in much quantity. Australian records, given the substantial incidence of transportation and assisted passage emigration, can be a valuable genealogical source.

Official passenger lists have been kept in the US since 1820, as Customs Passenger Lists from 1820 and as Immigration Passenger Lists from 1883. These records are in the National Archives in Washington. Lists for some US ports from 1820 up to 1865 are available in microform in the National Library of Ireland (see lists in *Tracing Your Irish Ancestors* by J. Grenham, 1992). A segment of passenger lists has been published in *The Famine Immigrants: lists of Irish Immigrants arriving at the Port of New York, 1846-1851,* 7 volumes, Baltimore,

US, 1983-86, and are widely available in reference libraries. These illustrate both the potential value and serious limitations of early passenger lists. If an emigrant ancestor or ancestor group are authoritatively believed to have emigrated during the Famine and do not have a common surname or if the names of the family group are known, then there is a reasonable chance that they will be found among the New York immigrants. But they could, of course, have disembarked in Boston or Philadelphia or have entered the US via Canada!

Emigration Trails and Emigration Schemes

An excellent source guide to the history of the Irish in the US is Patrick J. Blessing's *The Irish in America: a guide to the literature and the manuscript collections,* Washington, D.C., 1992. The definitive history of Irish emigration to North America is Kerby A. Miller's *Emigrants and Exiles: Ireland and the Irish exodus to North America,* 1985, paperback 1988, and valuable and provocative insights into the Irish emigrant experience are provided by D. H. Akenson's *Small Differences: Irish Catholics and Irish Protestants 1815-1922,* 1988, paperback 1991 and *The Irish Diaspora,* 1993, paperback 1995.

Source material for two emigration schemes to North America from County Cork merits mention, even though it represents only a minute fraction of total emigration. In 1823 and 1825, Peter Robinson supervised the emigration of over 2,500 people, mostly drawn from the Blackwater Valley in North Cork, to Upper Canada (now Ontario). The primary sources for what is known as the Robinson Settlements are the Peter Robinson papers, which are in Peterborough Public Library, Ontario. A microfilm copy of these papers is held by Cork County Library, which also holds a microfilm copy of H. T. Pammett's MA thesis (1934) on the Robinson emigration. Secondary material on the Robinson emigration is listed below.

A Famine emigration scheme from the Crown Estate of Kingwilliamstown (Ballydesmond) in Duhallow is documented in 'State-aided Emigration Schemes from Crown Estates in Ireland, c. 1850', ed. E. Ellis in *Analecta Hibernica,* No. 22. The article contains notes on the emigration scheme and lists 191 persons who emigrated from the Kingwilliamstown estate. A number of them settled in Buffalo and New York. The details provided are genealogically relevant, i.e., ages, relationship, etc.

As might be expected, some patterns of emigrant settlement within North America developed among emigrants from particular regions of County Cork and these can be of help to the family historian. In *The Irish lumberman-farmer,* 1982, the late Joseph King, using as a case-study his own Fitzgerald and Harrigan ancestors from the Mizen Peninsula in West Cork, documented a pattern of emigration and settlement in North America, which he called the Northern Migration Route. This emigrant trail, involving a period of settlement in New Brunswick, Canada, before spreading into and beyond the Great Lakes States of the US, was not untypical of pre-Famine emigration trends from County Cork. It is also the subject of his later *Ireland to North America,* 1994 and *The uncounted Irish in Canada and the US,* 1990. New Brunswick had a significant County Cork-born population in the nineteenth century. Among Cork settlements there was New Bandon, founded by 70 Methodists who emigrated from Bandon, County Cork in 1818 (D. F. Parrott & N. Hickey, 'New Bandon, New Brunswick', in *Bandon Historical Journal,* No. 7, 1991).

An occupational emigration pattern is identified and documented from parish records and local traditions in *Who were my ancestors?,* a series of community family histories compiled and published by Riobard O'Dwyer for the Beara peninsula in West Cork. The decline of copper mines in Allihies in Beara resulted in extensive migration by local families to Montana where their experience served them in the copper mines of Butte and other copper town in Montana. O'Dwyer's compilations are unique in Irish genealogical source material and are a valuable source for the genealogy of Beara emigrants in Montana and elsewhere in the US. For further details on the work of O'Dwyer, see Miscellaneous Sources chapter.

A further Cork-US emigrant trail is documented in *Duhallow to Oregon — 1880 to 1960,* by Marie Kelleher, Cork, c. 1988. Over several generations, young men from the Duhallow region of County Cork emigrated to Oregon where they engaged in sheep-farming. The establishment of a school of Emigration Studies at University College Cork at time of writing will hopefully lead to the identification of further patterns of emigration from County Cork to North America and will help to develop a synthesis of genealogical research and emigration studies.

From 1831 to 1916 a column entitled 'Missing Friends' was published in the *Boston Pilot* newspaper, providing a service to its readers that might enable them to re-establish contact with relatives or friends who had preceded them as emigrants or who had moved in search of work and lost contact. The publication since 1988 by New England Historic Genealogical Society of these notices under the title *The Search for Missing Friends* provides not only a valuable source for emigration studies, but also a source well worthy of perusal by family historians. These notices regularly contained the key elements required in a genealogical search, viz., parish, and frequently townland, of origin, age, names of siblings, etc. To date, five volumes have been published which cover all the 'Missing Friends' notices for the years 1831 to 1865. They are particularly relevant for those seeking Cork ancestors because almost ten percent of the 'missing friends' were natives of County Cork. This, of course, is simply a reflection of the many thousands who emigrated from Cork during that period, but those fortunate to identify a person named in the notices will usually have made a major step forward in their research. The published volumes are comprehensively indexed under person and place and have scholarly and informative introductory essays.

Realistically, the aforementioned sources will be of value to only a small proportion of those trying to chase down their County Cork ancestry. A preliminary question that family historians should pose themselves concerns their degree of certainty that they have a Cork ancestor. From 1860, Queenstown in Cork Harbour was the principal port of emigration for the majority of Irish emigrants from the southern half of Ireland and even further afield. This could have given rise to an erroneous family tradition of having 'come' from Cork. The strategy outlined in the 'Preliminaries' chapter is equally important for the overseas researcher. If you embark on an Irish search with little idea of an ancestors place of origin other than County Cork, it is unlikely that you will have any success.

However, it is very possible that you can do further research at home which will furnish you with the information you need. As with all genealogical research in Ireland, it is particularly important that you determine the name of the parish, and, if possible, the name of the locality within that parish, from which your County Cork ancestor emigrated. Determining the parish is so important, because there is no county-wide index to births, marriages or deaths for the years before 1864; and even after that date, it is often very difficult to be certain that one has found the person one is looking for.

To determine what parish your ancestor(s) came from, we suggest that you do the following:

• Ask the oldest of your relatives if they have ever heard of the place in County Cork your ancestors came from. Establish which ancestors in the country of adoption were of Irish birth and document their settlement pattern.

• Obtain copies of the death certificates of any ancestor born in County Cork to see if his or her place of birth is given in the record. If you know the names of your ancestor's brothers and sisters, obtain certificates for them as well. (Your local librarian will be able to tell you how to obtain birth, marriage and death certificates in your state or province). Take down the exact date of birth, if given.

• Locate the naturalisation (citizenship) record of your ancestor; the exact place of birth is sometimes given in this record. (Your local librarian can tell you what court has such records).

• Locate the grave-stones of any ancestors born in County Cork to see if the exact place of birth is inscribed on the stone.

• Determine where your ancestor was living at the time of a national census and find the entry for your ancestor's entire family. The exact place of foreign birth is not generally given, but you will then know the names of all persons in the family who were born in Ireland. Generally speaking it is probable that all members of the family were born in the same place if all are listed as born in Ireland. Take down the exact dates of birth, if given. (Your local librarian can tell you the dates national censuses were taken and where you can obtain the records).

• Make a list of all the persons you are reasonably sure were born in County Cork, with their approximate birth dates. Since certain family names tend to be more common in certain areas than others, you may be able to narrow down the area in which you hope to find your ancestors' birthplace. Thus, if your great-grandparents were James Murphy (a very common name in many County Cork parishes) and Bridget Jeffords (a much less common name), it may be possible to determine where the name Jeffords was found in considerable numbers. If you know that Bridget had a brother who married a Jeremiah Drinan before he left Ireland, and a sister who married a Bartholomew Scannell there, you have added two more names to your list. If you find James' and Bridget's parents' names in their death records, you will know the two surnames of their mothers. It may also be possible to determine the names of godparents or friends who 'came over' with your ancestors.

• At this point, it would be very useful to consult the microfilmed edition of the large scale survey of householders made for all of Ireland in the mid-nineteenth century (see Griffith's *Valuation* chapter). In a search of Griffith's, the occurrence of one very rare surname or a few fairly rare names in your family tree, can mean that this method is the most likely one to result in your finding your ancestors.

• Another useful source that can be consulted at this stage is Casey's fifteen volume compilation *O'Kief Coshe Mang etc.*, mainly dealing with North Cork, but also including general material relating to the entire county and adjacent areas. These volumes are widely available in larger libraries with an Irish studies collection. (The Albert E. Casey collection of Irish materials is housed in Samford University special collections Harwell G. Davis Library, Birmingham Alabama 35209.)

The Australian of Irish descent seeking genealogical data about a Cork ancestor can more reasonably expect to find relevant information on the ancetor's place of origin in state and national archives, whether that ancestor was free or convict, assisted or unassisted. The range of sources, their location and interpretation are beyond the scope of this book but are well-documented in Australian genealogical sources.

We hope that these suggestions will enable you to continue your search for your ancestors exact place of origin.

References

The Search for Missing Friends: Irish immigrant advertisements placed in the 'Boston Pilot' edited by Ruth-Ann Harris, B. Emer O'Keeffe et al., five volumes, Boston: NEHGS, 1989-
Valda Strauss: 'Irish Famine Orphans in Australia' in *Mallow Field Club Journal,* No. 11, 1993
Trevor McClaughlin, ed.: *Barefoot and Pregnant?: Irish famine orphans in*

Australia: Documents and Register, Melbourne, 1991
Christy Roche, 'Mallow and the Robinson Settlements' in *Mallow Field Club Journal,* No. 8, 1990
F. T. Frankling, 'Brief Background for Robinson Settlements', in *Mallow Field Club Journal,* No. 12, 1994

Chapter 4   Administrative Divisions

Records that are used for genealogical purposes today were originally compiled for other reasons: religious, administrative, taxation. The main compiling bodies were central and local government and the various churches. These organisations, operating over a very long time period, used a variety of administrative divisions. Before proceeding to an examination of the records themselves, then, it would be worthwhile having a brief look at the administrative geography of Cork.

The **townland** is the smallest, most important, and possibly most ancient Irish administrative division; there are 5,429 in County Cork. The term has nothing to do with a town. Townlands originated so long ago that it is not clear now what their original purpose was. It may be that they marked out territories belonging to particular families or family groupings. The average townland is about 350 acres (about 140 hectares) in size. Some are much bigger than this, some much smaller. Those composed of poor quality land tend to be bigger, those made up of good land tend to be smaller. It is as if an effort was made to divide land into parcels of equal value. Townland boundaries generally coincide with physical and man-made features such as roads, rivers, streams, hedges, walls, ditches, ridges and such. Some of these features may have disappeared over time. Often, these boundaries are not obvious and only residents with good local knowledge will be aware of them. Anybody else will require an Ordnance Survey map with a minimum scale of six inches to the mile, and a good eye, to locate a townland. Right up to the present time, the main component of the postal address of people who live outside a town or village, is the townland. All other territorial divisions are combinations of townlands, though sometimes a townland may be split between two of these other units.

Next in size and similar in antiquity is the **Parish**. Originally, this was an ecclesiastical territorial unit and it designated an area which was under the care of a clergyman and from whose inhabitants the clergyman drew an income of some sort. Because of this financial dimension the boundaries of parishes were fairly resistant to change, but changes did take place and they are of significance to researchers. When the Normans came to Ireland in the twelfth century, this parish structure was already in existence and they did little to alter it. During the Reformation of the sixteenth century, the Catholic Church in Ireland was suppressed. The Church of Ireland was established as the official church and ecclesiastical property was handed over to it. This new church maintained the old parish structure intact. As the official church, the Church of Ireland had some important functions to perform which these days would be considered to be the function of local government or the civil power. The Church of Ireland, for example, collected a local tax called the tithe, probated wills, conducted various official surveys, and registered burials. Their parishes, therefore, had a civil as well as a religious dimension and these units became known as **Civil Parishes**. The boundaries of civil parishes were marked on early Ordnance Survey maps, and the civil parishes were used as census divisions in the last century. With the passage of time, the Church of Ireland was gradually stripped of all civil powers and became simply a religious organisation. Its small membership encouraged a tendency to combine its parishes into larger units so that most of them became amalgamations of several civil parishes. **Church of Ireland Parishes**, therefore, became distinct from civil parishes.

The majority of the people in Ireland did not accept the religious changes of the sixteenth century and remained loyal to Rome. From the Reformation to the beginning of the nineteenth century there were periods of religious persecution of varying intensity which prevented the Catholic Church from organising itself along normal parochial lines. After Catholic Emancipation in 1829 had freed the Catholic Church from almost all the limitations that had been imposed on it, a new Catholic parish system was built up. However, in this revival, the ancient parish structure was often ignored and the new **Catholic Parishes** were organised to suit the needs of the people at the time. The new towns and villages, the density of the population and county boundaries were factors that influenced the shape of these new Catholic parishes.

In brief, the term parish can, therefore, have three meanings: a civil parish, of which there are 253 in Cork city and county, is an early ecclesiastical unit which became an administrative unit for civil purposes also; a Church of Ireland parish, of which there were about 190 in Cork in the middle of the nineteenth century, is usually a combination or union of civil parishes used by the Church of Ireland as a unit of organisation; a Catholic parish, of which there were 102 in Cork in 1880, is the unit of organisation set up by the Catholic Church after a long period of suppression.

For ecclesiastical purposes, Church of Ireland and Catholic parishes are grouped into **Dioceses**. A diocese is the area under the jurisdiction of a bishop. Catholic and Church of Ireland dioceses are very similar in outline but are not coterminous. Three dioceses fall fully or almost fully within the county of Cork: the dioceses of Cork, Cloyne and Ross. Parts of some border areas of Cork belong to dioceses which lie mostly outside of Cork: the dioceses of Kerry, Limerick, and Waterford & Lismore all impinge to some extent on County Cork.

The **Barony** is another important unit of territory as far as the genealogist is concerned. Its origins are also shrouded in mystery. Some claim that baronies were early Irish kingdoms. Another view states that it was the Normans who were responsible for these units and that the term means an area appropriate to the jurisdiction of a Baron. The barony is a much larger unit than a parish, but its shape and size seems to be rather random. Cork has 23 baronies. This unit was used by local government in collecting local taxation up to 1898, and it served as a census division up to 1901. It is still important as a reference for the location and identification of property.

When we come to discuss the **Poor Law Union** we are on firmer ground as far as its history is concerned, since it is of relatively recent origin. The Poor Law Act was passed in 1838 and it provided for the relief of the poor in Ireland by means of a workhouse system. In order to receive state assistance, the destitute had to commit themselves to a workhouse. Workhouses were to be provided right throughout Ireland and they were to be paid for by the levying of a local tax. For these purposes, the country was divided into units called poor law unions. Each union was to consist of a market town — in which the workhouse was to be built — and all the territory within about fifteen miles radius of the town. Those living within the union had to pay for the building and upkeep of the workhouse. They also had the power to elect a board of guardians whose function was to administer the system within the union.

Eventually, 163 poor law unions were formed. It was hoped that these new divisions would follow the boundaries of the existing parishes, baronies and counties, but that proved to be optimistic. In practice, the boundaries of both baronies and parishes were ignored, and even those of counties were not always respected. County Cork contains 15 poor law unions wholly within its borders, but three more are shared by the adjoining counties of Limerick, Tipperary and Waterford. No townland, however, is split between poor law unions. The integrity of the townland was required by the poor law legislation. This is not so as far as baronies and parishes are concerned. Though townlands do not generally tend to straddle barony and parish borders, they do so in a significant number of cases: two in every hundred townlands are split between two parishes.

Boards of guardians were to be elected by the ratepayers of each poor law union. For these purposes, each union was subdivided into **Electoral Divisions**. Again, each electoral divisions was to consist of a number of whole townlands. In 1898 the name of this territorial unit was changed to **District Electoral Division**. With the passage of time, this unit has increased in importance. Today, it is the basic unit for delineating constituencies in local and national elections,

Further social legislation in 1851 led to the establishment of other genealogically important divisions based on the poor law union. In that year the various boards of guardians were required to divide their unions into **Dispensary Districts** and to appoint a medical officer to each such district. A dispensary district was to consist of a number of whole electoral divisions. These districts became **Registrar's Districts** in 1864 with the introduction of civil registration of births, deaths and marriages. The medical officer became the registrar and had the duty of registering births, deaths and marriages that took place in his district. The clerk of the poor law union became a superintendent registrar.

In summary: a poor law union normally consisted of a market town, in which a workhouse was built, and the surrounding area of perhaps 170 square miles. This territory would be composed of whole townlands grouped into electoral divisions; these electoral divisions would be further grouped into larger divisions called both dispensary districts and registrar's districts.

These, then, are the main administrative divisions you are likely to encounter in your genealogical researches. If you find them somewhat confusing, there is no need to worry about that. As we examine different kinds of records in the chapters which follow, these matters will become much clearer.

Civil Parishes

Of all the administrative divisions mentioned above, the civil parish is possibly the most useful from a genealogical point of view. It is large enough to register on a small-scale map, it is the administrative unit on the basis of which many genealogically significant records were compiled, and it is not too difficult to relate it to other significant divisions such as barony, Catholic parish and Church of Ireland parish. The townland is too small to mark with any accuracy on a manageable map and there are too many of them in Cork to deal with individually, while the barony is too big to be of much use.

The following table, **Table 1**, consists of an alphabetical list of, and some important information concerning, all the civil parishes in County Cork — including the city parishes — a total of 253. This is more than ten per cent of all the civil parishes in Ireland — another indication of the relative largeness of Cork compared to other counties. The list is based on *Directory of Townlands and District Electoral Divisions*, published in 1985 by Cork County Council. All spellings are the 'official' spellings. They do not always coincide with either popular or modern usage. Some civil parishes in Cork have the same name; there are two of each of the following: Cullen, Donaghamore, Kilmeen and Kilquane.

The map references in column two key each parish name to one of the three accompanying maps, so it should be possible to pinpoint the location of each one. Whereas it would have been more convenient to use a single map for the county, Cork is so big that it was not possible to do so. Map reference numbers commencing with the letter *N* refer to map no. 1 — Cork North-West; references commencing with the letter *E* refer to map no. 2 — Cork East; references commencing with the letter *S* refer to map no. 3 — Cork South-West. Two and sometimes even three map references are given for some parishes. This simply means that the parishes are on the borderline between the maps and may be located on more than one map.

It will be immediately apparent from these maps that civil parishes vary greatly in size and that their boundaries follow no geometrical design. The maps have the appearance of jigsaw puzzles. Another strange feature that becomes apparent with a little study of the maps is that some civil parishes have 'islands', i.e., separate, detached pieces which may be a considerable distance apart from one another; Macroom, which is split into three pieces, is an example of this phenomenon. The city parishes of St Finbar, St Anne Shandon and St Nicholas all have islands. There are historical reasons for this which need not concern us here. Sometimes the parishes that are split are divided between different Catholic or Church of Ireland parishes, as, indeed, are several other parishes that are not split.

Column three gives the date of the tithe applotment book — it should be noted that, in some cases no tithe applotment book is available, while there are several available for other parishes: four for Kilmocomoge, for example. If the name of the parish is in **bold**, that means that a tithe defaulters list is also available for that parish (see the chapter on tithe applotment books).

The fourth column lists the name or names of the Catholic parish or parishes in which the civil parish was situated in the year 1875. This information is based, for the most part, on Guy's *County and City of Cork Directory for the Years 1875-1876*, and, in the case of the dioceses of Cloyne, on the work of Canon B. Troy, Parish Priest of Midleton.

Column five names the Church of Ireland parish/parishes in which the civil parish was situated in 1863. This information is based on what may be gleaned from Rev. J. H. Cole's *Church and Parish Records of the United Diocese of Cork, Cloyne and Ross*, published in 1903, on Guy's 1875 directory to which reference has already been made, and on local knowledge.

It is important to remember that over the centuries ecclesiastical parishes, both Catholic and Church of Ireland, expanded, contracted, split in two, amalgamated and occasionally changed in name. These factors make it very difficult to locate each parish accurately within its Catholic or Church of Ireland parish, so a certain amount of guess work had to be employed in the compilation of Table 1. Even if the table were absolutely accurate for the dates given — 1875 for Catholic parishes and 1863 for Church of Ireland parishes — a few decades before or a few decades later, the position would have been somewhat different, albeit marginally so.

Samuel Lewis's *A Topographical Dictionary of Ireland* is a book worth consulting for further information on civil parishes. This work, in two volumes, is available in well-stocked libraries. It was first published in 1837 and reprinted several times subsequently. It gives a description of all the civil parishes in Ireland — arranged alphabetically — and in most cases names the Catholic and Church of Ireland parish in which the civil parish was situated at that time.

The final column headed 'Notes' identifies all those parishes which are composed of two or more pieces and also indicates whether the pieces are close together or far apart. This should be of some assistance in locating those parishes on the maps.

Table 1

Civil Parish	Map	TAB	Catholic Parish	Church of Irl Parish	Notes
Abbeymahon	S66	1834	Timoleague	Abbeymahon	
Abbeystrowry	S52	1835	Skibbereen, Aghadown	Abbeystrewry	2 parts, close
Aghabulloge	N48	1827	Coachford, Aghinagh	Aghabulloge	
Aghacross	E32a	1826	Kildorrery	Doneraile	
Aghada	E105	1828	Aghada	Aghada	
Aghadown	S55	1828	Aghadown	Aghadown	
Aghern	E69	1824	Conna	Ahern	
Aghinagh	N50	1833	Aghinagh, Macroom	Ahinagh	
Aglish	N56	1825/43	Ovens	Aglish	
Aglishdrinagh	N24	1827	Ballyhay	Aglishdrinagh	2 parts, close
Ardagh	E87	1828	Killeagh	Ardagh	
Ardfield	S61	1824	Ardfield	Ardfield	2 parts, close
Ardnageehy	E42	1826	Watergrasshill	Ardnageehy	
Ardskeagh	E2	1833	Ballyhay	Ballyhay	
Athnowen	N57	1827	Ovens	Athnowen	
Ballinaboy	E85, N70, S25	1833	Ballinhassig	Ballinaboy	
Ballinadee	N46, S74	1826	Courceys	Ballinadee	2 parts, distant
Ballintemple	E108	1833/34	Cloyne	Cloyne	

Civil Parish	Map	TAB	Catholic Parish	Church of Irl Parish	Notes
Ballyclogh	N34	1831	Ballyclogh, Castlemagner	Ballyclough	
Ballycurrany	E53	1826	Lisgoold	Carrigtohill	
Ballydeloher	E59	1833	Glounthane	Killaspugmullane	
Ballydeloughy	E12	1825	Glanworth	Brigown	
Ballyfeard	S29	1827/34	Clontead	Ballyfeard	
Ballyfoyle	S35	1833	Tracton	Nohaval	
Ballyhay	N20, E1	1833	Ballyhay	Ballyhay	4 parts, close
Ballyhooley	E27	1833	Castletownroche	Ballyhooly	
Ballymartle	S26	1824/36	Clontead	Ballymartle	
Ballymodan	S20	1832	Bandon	Ballymodan	
Ballymoney	S70	**1833**	Desert, Dunmanway	Ballymoney	
Ballynoe	E70	1833	Conna	Ballynoe	
Ballyoughtera	E94	1833	Midleton, Cloyne	Castlemartyr	2 parts, distant
Ballyspillane	E62	1833	Midleton	Midleton	
Ballyvourney	N38	**1827**	B.vourney, Kilnamartyra	Ballyvourney	
Barnahely	S41	1830/34	Passage West	Carrigaline	
Bohillane	E99	1833	Ballymacoda	Bohillane	
Bregoge	N31	1833	Buttevant	Buttevant	
Bridgetown	E25	1825	Castletownroche	Bridgetown	
Brigown	E33	1830	Mitchelstown	Brigown	
Brinny	S17	1834	Innishannon	Brinny	
Britway	E50	1826	Castlelyons	Ahern	2 parts, close
Buttevant	N32	1833	Buttevant	Buttevant	
Caheragh	S46	1827	Caheragh	Caheragh	2 parts, close
Caherduggan	E8	1828	Doneraile	Buttevant	
Caherlag	E60	1833	Glounthane, Glanmire	Rathcooney	2 parts, close
Cannaway	N55	1833/34	Kilmurry	Cannaway	
Carrigaline	E84,S38	1827/31	Carrigaline, Douglas	Carrigaline	2 parts, close
Carrigdownane	E13	1833	Kildorrery	Carrigdownane	
Carrigleamleary	E15	1831	Anakissy	Carrigamleary	
Carrigrohane	E78, N64	1829	Ballincollig	Carrigrohane	
Carrigrohanebeg	N58	1824	Inniscarra	Carrigrohanebeg	
Carrigtohill	E61	1834	Carrigtwohill	Carrigtohill	2 parts, close
Castlehaven	S53	1825	Castlehaven	Castlehaven	
Castlelyons	E44	1824/26	Castlelyons	Castlelyons	2 parts, close
Castlemagner	N10	1833/34	Castlemagner	Castlemagner	
Castletownroche	E17	1826/26	Castltownroche	Castletownroche	
Castleventry	S13	1833/34	Kilmeen	Kilkerranmore	3 parts, close
Christ Church	*see* Holy Trinity				
Churchtown	N27	1833	Liscarrol, Freemount	Churchtown	2 parts, distant
Clear Island	S58	1833/35	Rath and the Islands	Kilcoe	
Clenor	E16	1831/32	Anakissy	Clenore	
Clondrohid	N39	**1834**	Clondrohid, Macroom	Clondrohid	
Clondulane	E38a	1828	Fermoy	Clondulane	1851 census
Clonfert	N1	1826	Kantk, Newmkt, Meelin	Clonfert	
Clonmeen	N13	1825/36	Castlemagner	Clonmeen	
Clonmel	E66	1824	Queenstown	Clonmel	
Clonmult	E58	1831	Imogeela	Clonmult	
Clonpriest	E91	**1833**	Youghal, Killeagh	Clonpriest	
Clontead	S84	1833	Clontead	Ballymartle, Kinsale	
Cloyne	E98	1833/34	Cloyne	Cloyne	4 parts, close
Coole	E45	1829	Castleloyns	Coole	
Cooliney	N23	1834	Ballyhay	Ballyhay	

Civil Parish	Map	TAB	Catholic Parish	Church of Irl Parish	Notes
Corbally	N66	1833	Ballincollig	Carrigrohane	
Corcomohide	N18	1829	Ballyagran	Corcomohide	
Cork City Parishes	E80	*see* Holy Trinity, Ss. Paul's and St Peter's			
Corkbeg	E107	1834	Aghada	Corkbeg	
Creagh	S56	**1831**	Skibbereen	Creagh	2 parts close
Cullen (Duhallow)	N11	1825/34	Drishane	Dromtarriff	2 separate
Cullen (Kinalea)	S27	1825	Clontade	Cullen	parishes
Currykippane	E75	1827	St Mary's (N. Cathedral)	Carrigrohane	
Dangandonovan	E88	1827	Killeagh	Dingindonavan	
Derryvillane	E11	1825	Glanworth	Derryvillane	
Desert	S79	1833	Clonakilty	Kilgariffe	
Desertmore	N61	1833	Ovens	Desertmore	
Desertserges	S71	1829	Desert	Desartserges	
Donaghmore (Barony of Ibane & Barryroe)	S68	1833	Timoleague	Donaghmore	
Donaghmore (Barony of Muskerry)	N49	1827	Donoughmore	Donoughmore	
Doneraile	E5	1833	Doneraile	Doneraile	
Drinagh	S51	1833	Drimoleague	Drinagh	
Drishane	N36	**1831**	Drishane	Dromtarriff	
Dromdaleague	S50	1826	Drimoleague	Drimoleague	
Dromdowney	N35	N/A	Ballyclogh	Castlemagner	
Dromtarriff	N12	1827	Dromtarriff	Dromtarriff	
Dunbulloge	E41	1824	Glanmire	Dunbulloge	
Dunderrow	S24, N68	1825	Ballinhassig	Dunderrow	2 parts, distant
Dungourney	E57	1824	Imogeela	Dungourney	
Dunisky	N44	1833	Kilmichael	Cannaway	
Dunmahon	E20	1831	Glanworth	Kilworth	
Durrus	S45	1830	Muintervara	Durrus & Kilcrohane	
Fanlobbus	S9	1826	Dunmanway	Fanlobbus	
Farahy	E7	1831	Kildorrery	Farrihy	
Fermoy	E38	1834	Fermoy	Fermoy	
Garranekinnefeake	E97	1834	Aghada	Garrane-Kinnefeake	
Garrycloyne	N54	1834	Blarney	Garrycloyne	
Garryvoe	E100	1834	Ballymacoda	Castlemartyr	
Glanworth	E18	1827	Glanworth	Glanworth	2 parts, close
Gortroe	E49	1825	Rathcormac	Gortroe & Dysart	
Grenagh	N72	1834	Grenagh	Garrycloyne	
Hackmys	N22	1833	Ballyhay	Ballyhay	
Holy Trinity	E80		St Peter & Paul's	Holy Trinity	
Ightermurragh	E95	**1833**	Ballymacoda	Ightermurragh	
Imphrick	E4, N29	1825	Ballyhay	Buttevant	
Inch	E103	1833	Aghada, Cloyne	Inch	3 parts, distant
Inchigeelagh	N42, S6	1827-34	Iveleary	Inchigeela	
Inchinabacky	E65	1833	Midleton	Inchinabacky	
Inishannon	S22	1823/30/40	Innishannon	Innishannon	
Inishcarra	N52	1827	Inniscarra	Inniscarra	
Inishkenny	E83, N69	1825	Ballincollig	Inniskenny	
Island	S62	1833	Clonakilty	Kilgariffe	8 parts, distant
Kilbolane	N17	1830	Freemount	Churchtown	
Kilbonane	N60	1825	Kilmurry	Kilbonane	
Kilbrin	N7	1832/39	Ballyclogh, Castlemagner	Kilbrin	
Kilbrittain	S73	1833	Kilbrittain	Kilbrittain	

Civil Parish	Map	TAB	Catholic Parish	Church of Irl Parish	Notes
Kilbrogan	S19	1827	Bandon	Kilbrogan	
Kilbroney	N30	1833	Buttevant	Buttevant	
Kilcaskan	S2	1827	Kilkaskin South	Berehaven	
Kilcatherine	S1	1827	Kilcatherine	Berehaven	
Kilcoe	S48	1830	Aghadown	Kilcoe	
Kilcorcoran	N6	1829	Kanturk	Ballyclough	
Kilcorney	N37	1825	Clonmeen	Kilcorney	
Kilcredan	E101	1828/34	Ballymacoda	Kilcredan	
Kilcrohane	S44	1831	Muinteravara	Durrus	
Kilcrumper	E21	1828	Fermoy, Kilworth	Kilworth 1851 census; 2 parts, close	
Kilcully	E74	1826	Upper Glanmire	Kilcully	
Kilcummer	E26	1825	Castletownroche	Castletownroche	
Kildorrery	E30	**1834**	Kildorrery	Farrihy	
Kilfaughnabeg	S14	1829	Kilmacabea	Kilfaughnabeg	
Kilgarriff	S75	1833	Clonakilty	Kilgariff	
Kilgrogan	N28	N/A	Liscarroll		
Kilgullane	E34	1825	Glanworth	Brigown	2 parts, close
Kilkerranmore	S59	1833	Rosscarbery, Kilmeen	Kilkerranemore	
Killaconenagh	S4	1833	Kilaconenagh	Berehaven	
Killanully	E86, S39	1833	Douglas	Killanully	
Killaspugmullane	E51	1826	Watergrasshill	Killaspugmullane	
Killathy	E28	1833/34	Castletownroche	Ballyhooly	
Killeagh	E90	**1833**	Killeagh	Killeagh	
Killeenemer	E19	1827	Glanworth	Killeenemer	
Killowen	S18	1834	Murragh	Killowen	
Kilmacabea	S11	1829	Kilmacabea	Kilmacabea	
Kilmacdonagh	E96	1834	Ballymacoda	Castlemartyr	
Kilmaclenine	N33	1827	Ballyclogh	Kilmaclenine	
Kilmahon	E104	1833	Ballymacoda, Cloyne	Kilmahon	2 parts, close
Kilmaloda	S72	1826	Timoleague	Kilmaloda	
Kilmeen (Carbery)	S10	1829	Kilmeen (Ross)	Kilmeen	2 separate
Kilmeen (Duhallow)	N5	1834	Kilmeen (Kerry)	Dromtarriff	parishes
Kilmichael	N45, S7	1826/34	Kilmichael	Kilmichael	
Kilmocomoge	S5	1825-35	Bantry	Kilmocomoge	4 TABs
Kilmoe	S49	1828	Schull (West)	Kilmoe	
Kilmoney	S42	1834	Carrigaline	Carrigaline	
Kilmonoge	S32	1825/35	Clountead	Nohaval	
Kilmurry	N47	1834	Kilmichael	Kilmurry	
Kilnaglory	E82, N63	1827	Ballincollig	Athnowen	
Kilnagross	S77	1827	Clonakilty	Kilnagross	
Kilnamanagh	S3	1827	Kilnamanagh	Berehaven	
Kilnamartery	N40	1826	Kilnamartery, Macroom	Kilnamartery	
Kilpatrick	S31	1833	Tracton	Nohaval	2 parts, close
Kilphelan	E35	1833	Glanworth	Brigown	2 parts, distnt
Kilquane (Barrymore)	E52	1826	Glounthane	Killaspugmullane	2 separate
Kilquane (Fermoy)	E3	1834	Ballyhay	Ballyhay	parishes
Kilroan	S82	1834/39	Courceys	Kilroan	
Kilroe	N8	1833	Kanturk, Castlemagner	Kanturk	
Kilshanaghan	E48	1826	Watergrasshill	Killaspugmullane	
Kilshannig	N16	1823	Glantane	Kilshannick	
Kilsillagh	S69	1832	Timoleague	Lislee	
Kilworth	E36	1827/28	Kilworth	Kilworth	1851 census
Kinneigh	S8	1827/34	Murragh	Kinneigh	

Civil Parish	Map	TAB	Catholic Parish	Church of Irl Parish	Notes
Kinsale	S85	N/A	Kinsale	Kinsale	
Kinure	S33	1833	Kinsale	Kinsale	
Knockavilly	N67, S21	1827	Innishannon	Knockavilly	
Knockmourne	E68	1833	Conna	Knockmourne	
Knocktemple	N3	1831	Freemount	Knocktemple	
Lackeen	N26	1834	Liscarroll	Lackeen	
Leighmoney	S28	1827	Innishannon	Leighmoney	
Leitrim	E39	1827	Kilworth	Kilworth	1851 census
Liscarroll	N25	1833	Liscarroll	Kilbrin	
Liscleary	S40	1827	Douglas	Liscleary	2 parts, close
Lisgoold	E54	1826	Lisgoold	Lisgoold	
Lislee	S67	1833	Timoleague	Lislee	
Lismore & Mocollop	E40	1825	Lismore	Lismore	
Litter	E29	1834	Fermoy, Castletownroche	Litter	
Little Island	E63	1833	Glounthane	Rathcooney	
Macloneigh	N43	1827	Kilmichael	Inchigeela	
Macroney	E37	1827	Kilworth	Kilworth	1851 census
Macroom	N41	1827	Macroom	Macroom	4 parts distant
Magourney	N51	1833	Aghabulloge	Magourney	
Mallow	E14, N15	1823	Mallow	Mallow	
Marmullane	S36	1833	Passage West	Marmullane	
Marshalstown	E32	1831	Mitchelstown	Marshalstown	
Matehy	N53	1827	Grenagh, Inniscarra	Inniscarra	
Middleton	E93	1833	Midleton	Midleton	
Mogeely (Imokilly)	E89	1828	Imogeela	Castlemartyr	2 separate
Mogeely (Kinnataloon)	E71	1830	Conna	Mogeely	parishes
Mogeesha	E64	1834	Carrigtwohill	Mogeesha	
Monanimy	E24	1830	Anakissy	Monanimy	
Monkstown	S37	1834	Monkstown	Monkstown	
Mourneabbey	E22, N71	N/A	Mourne Abbey	Mourne Abbey	
Moviddy	N59	1826	Kilmurry	Moviddy	
Murragh	S15	1833	Murragh	Murragh	
Myross	S54	1829	Castlehaven	Myross	
Nohaval	S34	1826	Tracton	Nohaval	
Nohavaldaly	N4	1829/34	Kilmeen (Kerry)	Dromtarriff	
Rahan	E23	1825	Mourne Abbey, Mallow	Rahan	
Rathbarry	S60	1833	Ardfield	Rathbarry	2 parts, close
Rathclarin	S78	1833	Kilbrittain	Rathclarin	
Rathcooney	E73	1826	Glanmire	Rathcooney	
Rathcormack	E43	1833	Rathcormac	Rathcormac	
Rathgoggan	N21	1833	Charleville	Ballyhay	
Ringcurran	S86	1828	Kinsale	Rincurran	2 parts, close
Ringrone	S81	1830	Courceys	Ringrone	2 parts, close
Roskeen	N14	1834	Castlemagner	Castlemagner	
Ross	S12	1834	Rosscarbery	Ross Cathedral	
Rostellan	E102	1825	Aghada	Rostellan	2 parts, close
St Anne's Shandon	E77	1830	St Mary's (N. Cathedral)	St Anne's Shandon	2 pts, close
St Finbar's	E79, N62	1827/28	St Finbar's/Ovens	St Finbarre's	2 parts, distant
St Mary's Shandon	E76	1833	St Mary's (N. Cathedral)	St Mary's Shandon	
St Michael's	E46	1825	Glanmire	Glanmire	
St Nathlash	E10	**1830**	Kildorrery	Nathlash	
St Nicholas	N65, E81	1834	St Finbar's (S. Parish)	St Nicholas	2 parts, distant
St Paul's	E80	N/A	St Peter & Paul's	St Paul's	

Contd. on p. 36

Map No 1: Cork North-West

Clonfert	N1	Ballyhea (4 pts)	N20	Clondrohid	N39	Carrigrohanebeg	N58
Tullylease	N2	Rathgoggan	N21	Kilnamartry	N40	Moviddy	N59
Knocktemple	N3	Hackmys	N22	Macroom (4 pts)	N41	Kilbonane	N60
Nohavaldaly	N4	Cooliney	N23	Inchigeelagh	N42	Desertmore	N61
Kilmeen	N5	Aglishdrinagh (2 pts)	N24	Maconleigh	N43	St Finbar's	N62
Kilcorcoran	N6	Liscarroll	N25	Dunisky	N44	Kilnagleary	N63
Kilbrin	N7	Lackeen	N26	Kilmichael	N45	Carrigrohane	N64
Kilroe	N8	Churchtown (2 pts)	N27	Ballinadee	N46	St Nicholas	N65
Subulter	N9	Kilgrogan	N28	Kilmurry	N47	Corbally	N66
Castlemagner	N10	Imphrick	N29	Aghabulloge	N48	Knockavilly	N67
Cullen	N11	Kilbroney	N30	Donaghmore	N49	Dunderrow	N68
Dromtarriff	N12	Bregoge	N31	Aghinagh	N50	Inishkenny	N69
Clonmeen	N13	Buttevant	N32	Magourney	N51	Ballinaboy	N70
Roskeen	N14	Kilmaclenan	N33	Inniscarra	N52	Mourne Abbey	N71
Mallow	N15	Ballyclogh	N34	Matehy	N53	Grenagh	N72
Kilshannig	N16	Dromdowney	N35	Garrycloyne	N54	Whitechurch	N73
Kilbolane	N17	Drishane	N36	Cannaway	N55		
Corcomohide	N18	Kilcorney	N37	Aglish	N56		
Shandrum	N19	Ballyvourney	N38	Athnowen	N57		

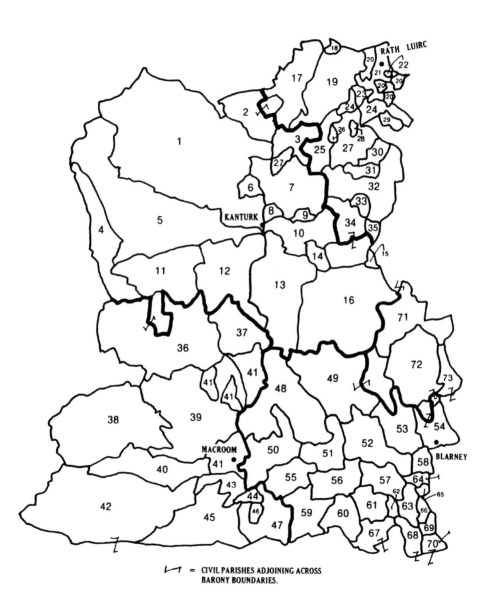

Map No. 1: Civil Parish Map of Cork North-West

Map No 2: Cork East

Ballyhea	E1	Litter	E29	Templebodan	E55	Inishkenny	E83
Ardskeagh	E2	Kildorrery	E30	Templenacarriga	E56	Carrigaline (2 pts)	E84
Kilquane	E3	Templemolaga	E31	Dungourney	E57	Ballinaboy (2 pts)	E85
Imphrick	E4	Marshalstown	E32	Clonmult	E58	Killanully	E86
Doneraile	E5	Aghacross	E32a	Ballydeloher	E59	Ardagh	E87
Templeroan	E6	Brigown	E33	Caherlag (2 pts)	E60	Dangandonovan	E88
Farahy	E7	Kilgullane (2pts)	E34	Carrigtohill (2 pts)	E61	Mogeely	E89
Caherduggan	E8	Kilphelan (2 pts)	E35	Ballyspillane	E62	Killeagh	E90
Wallstown	E9	Kilworth	E36	Little Island	E63	Clonpriest	E91
St Nathlash	E10	Macroney	E37	Mogeesha	E64	Youghal	E92
Derryvillane	E11	Fermoy	E38	Inchinabacky	E65	Midleton	E93
Ballydeloughy	E12	Clondulane	E38a	Clonmel	E66	Ballyoughtera (2 pts)	E94
Carrigdownane	E13	Leitrim	E39	Templerobin	E67	Ightermurragh	E95
Mallow	E14	Lismore & Mocollop	E40	Knockmourne	E68	Kilmacdonagh	E96
Carrigleamleary	E15	Dunbulloge	E41	Aghern	E69	Garranekinnefeake	E97
Clenor	E16	Ardnageehy	E42	Ballynoe	E70	Cloyne (4 pts)	E98
Castletownroche	E17	Rathcormack	E43	Mogeely	E71	Bohillane	E99
Glanworth (2 pts)	E18	Castlelyons (2 pts)	E44	Whitechurch	E72	Garryvoe	E100
Killeenemer	E19	Coole	E45	Rathcooney	E73	Kilcredan	E101
Dunmahon	E20	St Michael's	E46	Kilcully	E74	Rostellan (2 pts)	E102
Kilcrumper (2 pts)	E21	Templeusque	E47	Currykippane	E75	Inch (3 pts)	E103
Mournabbey	E22	Kilshanaghan	E48	St Mary's Shandon	E76	Kilmahon (2 pts)	E104
Rahan	E23	Gortroe	E49	St Ann's Shandon (2 pts)	E77	Aghada	E105
Monanimy	E24	Britway (2 pts)	E50	Carrigrohane	E78	Titeskin (2 pts)	E106
Bridgetown	E25	Killaspugmullane	E51	St Finbar's	E79	Corkbeg	E107
Kilcummer	E26	Kilquane	E52	Cork City Parishes	E80	Ballintemple	E108
Ballyhooley	E27	Ballycurrany	E53	St Nicholas	E81	Trabolgan	E109
Killathy	E28	Lisgoold	E54	Kilnagleary	E82		

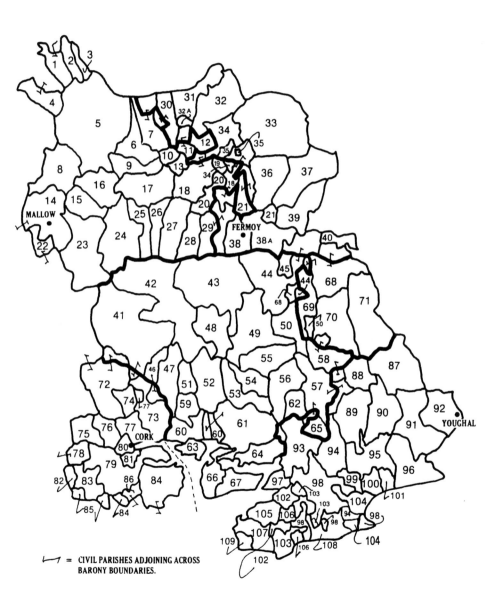

= CIVIL PARISHES ADJOINING ACROSS BARONY BOUNDARIES.

Map No. 2: Civil Parish Map of Cork East

Map No 3: Cork South-West

Kilcatherine	S1	Templemichael	S23	Durrus	S45	Lislee	S67
Kilcaskan	S2	Dunderrow (2 pts)	S24	Caheragh (2 pts)	S46	Donaghmore	S68
Kilnamanagh	S3	Ballinaboy	S25	Skull	S47	Kilsillagh	S69
Killaconenagh	S4	Ballymartle	S26	Kilcoe	S48	Ballymoney	S70
Kilmacomoge	S5	Cullen	S27	Kilmoe	S49	Desertserges	S71
Inchigeelagh	S6	Leighmoney	S28	Dromdaleague	S50	Kilmaloda	S72
Kilmichael	S7	Ballyfeard	S29	Drinagh	S51	Kilbrittain	S73
Kinneigh	S8	Tracton	S30	Abbeystrowry (2 pts)	S52	Ballinadee	S74
Fanlobbus	S9	Kilpatrick (2pts)	S31	Castlehaven	S53	Kilgarriff	S75
Kilmeen	S10	Kilmonoge	S32	Myross	S54	Templebryan (2 pts)	S76
Kilmacabea	S11	Kinure	S33	Aghadown	S55	Kilnagross	S77
Ross	S12	Nohaval	S34	Creagh (2 pts)	S56	Rathclarin	S78
Castleventry (3 pts)	S13	Ballyfoyle	S35	Tullagh	S57	Desert	S79
Kilfaughnabeg	S14	Marmullane	S36	Clear Island	S58	Templetrine	S80
Murragh	S15	Monkstown	S37	Kilkerranmore	S59	Ringrone (2 pts)	S81
Templemartin	S16	Carrigaline (2 pts)	S38	Rathbarry (2 pts)	S60	Kilroan	S82
Brinny	S17	Killanully	S39	Ardfield (2 pts)	S61	Tisaxon	S83
Killowen	S18	Liscleary (2 pts)	S40	Island (9 pts)	S62	Clontead	S84
Kilbrogan	S19	Barnahely	S41	Templeomalus	S63	Kinsale	S85
Ballymodan	S20	Kilmoney	S42	Templequinlan	S64	Ringcurran (2 pts)	S86
Knockavilly	S21	Templebreedy	S43	Timoleague	S65		
Inishannon	S22	Kilcrohane	S44	Abbeymahon	S66		

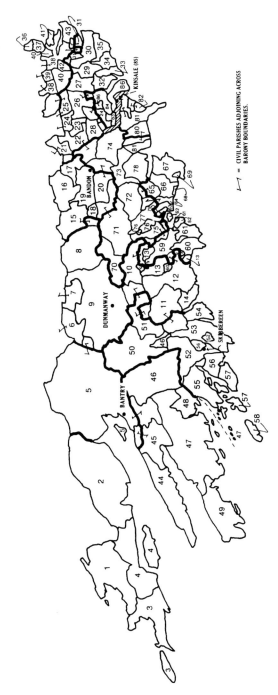

Map No. 3: Civil Parish Map of Cork South-West

Civil PARISH	Map	TAB	Catholic Parish	Church of Irl Parish	Notes
St Peter's	E80	N/A	St Peter & Paul's	St Peter's	
Shandrum	N19	1830	Shandrum	Shandrum	
Skull	S47	1827	Skull, East and West	Skull	
Subulter	N9	1834	Castlemagner	Subulter	
Templebodan	E55	1834	Lisgoold	Templebodan	
Templebreedy	S43	1833	Carrigaline	Templebreedy	
Templebryan	S76	1831/33	Clonakilty	Templebryan	
Templemartin	S16	1833	Desert	Templemartin	
Templemichael	S23	1826	Ballinhassig	Templemichael	
Templemolaga	E31	1826	Kildorrery	Doneraile	
Templenacarriga	E56	1833	Lisgoold	Templenacarriga	
Templeomalus	S63	1833	Clonakilty	Templeomalus	
Templequinlan	S64	1832/34	Clonakilty	Templequinlan	
Templeroan	E6	1829	Doneraile	Templeroan	
Templerobin	E67	1825	Queenstown	Clonmel	
Templetrine	S80	1833	Courceys	Templetrine	
Templeusque	E47	1828	Glanmire	Kilroan	
Timoleague	S65	1828	Timoleague	Timoleague	
Tisaxon	S83	1825	Kinsale	Taxax	
Titeskin	E106	1833	Aghada	Aghada	2 parts, close
Trabolgan	E109	1834	Aghada	Corkbeg	(TAB with Corkbeg)
Tracton	S30	1833	Tracton	Tracton	
Tullagh	S57	1829	Skibbereen, Rath	Tullagh	
Tullylease	N2	1828	Freemount	Tullilease	
Wallstown	E9	**1833/39**	Anakissy, Doneraile	Wallstown	
Whitechurch	E72, N73	1826	Blarney	Whitechurch	
Youghal	E92	1833	Youghal	Youghal	

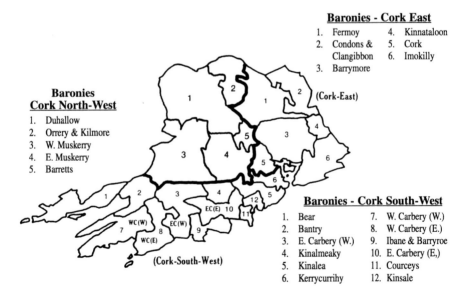

Baronies - Cork East

1. Fermoy   4. Kinnataloon
2. Condons &   5. Cork
   Clangibbon   6. Imokilly
3. Barrymore

(Cork-East)

Baronies Cork North-West

1. Duhallow
2. Orrery & Kilmore
3. W. Muskerry
4. E. Muskerry
5. Barretts

(Cork-South-West)

Baronies - Cork South-West

1. Bear   7. W. Carbery (W.)
2. Bantry   8. W. Carbery (E.)
3. E. Carbery (W.)   9. Ibane & Barryroe
4. Kinalmeaky   10. E. Carbery (E,)
5. Kinalea   11. Courceys
6. Kerrycurrihy   12. Kinsale

Chapter 5   Censuses

One important event that all researchers need to become acquainted with at an early stage is the destruction of the Public Record Office and its contents in 1922. Most people seem to hear about the genealogical treasures that lay within — such as the censuses of 1821, 1831, 1841, 1851, which virtually named every man, woman and child alive in Ireland during the first half of the nineteenth century — before they are told that everything was burnt up in the opening encounter of the Irish civil war in June 1922. On that day the men who thought they were making history destroyed the history of the ordinary Irish people. The 'short and simple annals of the poor' recorded in innumerable census forms during the previous hundred years, fell in the form of black ashes on the streets of Dublin, mingled with the ashes of other irreplaceable historical documents. Some would quibble with Winston Churchill's summing up of the catastrophe: 'Better a state without archives than archives without a State'.

Luckily, neither the 1901 nor the 1911 census returns were in the Public Record Office that day. They were stored locally and were saved from destruction. Both sets — complete for the whole country — are now public records and may be examined at the National Archives, Dublin. The 1901 census returns have been microfilmed — unlike those for 1911 — which ensures that they are available at several locations. The 1911 returns are still available only at the National Archives, though microfilming is currently in progress.

The 1901 and 1911 censuses required the following information to be recorded about each individual in a household: Name; Relation to the head of the family; Religion; Literacy; Age; Sex; Rank, profession or occupation; Marital status; Where born (if in Ireland, the county was to be named); Ability to speak Irish and English; Specified physical and mental disabilities. The 1911 census additionally required married women to give the following information: Number of years the current marriage has lasted; Total number of children born alive to present marriage; Total number of children still living.

In the National Archives, the 1901 census returns are bound together in large volumes and arranged in townland or street order. The returns for each townland or street are preceded by an enumerator's abstract giving some statistical information and also listing the heads of household in the returns that follow. The ease with which relevant census forms may be located depends on how specific your information is with regard to the address of the individual or family you are researching. If you know the townland or, in the case of town dwellers, the street, you should have no bother putting your hands on what you are looking for. First of all, you must consult the 1901 *General Alphabetical Index to the Townland and Towns of Ireland*, better known as *The Townland Index*. This lists Ireland's 60,000 townlands in alphabetical order. It gives the following information about each townland: the Ordnance Survey sheet number; the area in statute acres; the name of the county, barony, parish, county district and district electoral division in which it is situated. There is also a column headed 'No. in table vii in Census County Book, 1901'. This reference, plus the name of the county, will enable the staff at the National Archives to find the 1901 census volume you require.

Separate street indexes have been compiled for cities, Cork City included, and are available on open shelves at the reading room of the National Archives.

The 1911 census returns are not bound in volumes, they are available in boxes of loose sheets arranged in the same order as the 1901 census returns.

Fragments of the various 1821, 1831, 1841 and 1851 censuses survive for some parts of Ireland. The only County Cork portion to survive is from 1851 and relates to an area around Kilworth in North-East Cork. The surviving returns cover all of the civil parishes of Kilworth and Kilcrumper, most of Leitrim part of Macroney and one townland of Clondulane. These census records were published in the US in 1994 under the title *County Cork: a collection of 1851 census records* (ed. J. Masterson, published for Clearfield Co. by Genealogical Publishing, 1994, reprinted, 1996). The originals are in the National Archives. Cork County Library has a copy of another version of this census.

A series of documents based on information on the 1841 and 1851 censuses has survived intact. These documents are of some genealogical interest. In 1908, with the introduction of old age pensions, many people had difficulty in showing that they were entitled to this social benefit since they could not easily prove that they were over the requisite 70 years of age. The problem was that civil registration had not begun until 1864 so, some other way of certifying age was necessary. The checking of early census forms became a regular way of establishing age. An applicant sent his details to the Public Record Office; an official checked the census returns and if the applicant's name was found a certificate was issued, generally known as a 'green form', giving his name, age, parentage and birth place. These forms survived and are available in the National Archives. There is a census search form index for each county. The index is arranged by barony, civil parish and townland. The name of any person who had a search done on his behalf will appear under the name of the townland in which he lived.

Religious Censuses

At various times in the eighteenth and nineteenth centuries, returns of householders were made both at parochial and/or national level. While the specific reason behind these 'censuses' differed, they invariably had religious enumeration as a common link.

In 1766, Church of Ireland rectors were instructed to make a return of householders in their parishes indicating the religious persuasion of each household. While in some instances the rector supplied only numerical totals of Protestants and Catholics in his parish, the norm was a listing of the heads of household and the religion of the household members. These returns were almost totally destroyed in 1922 in the fire at the Public Record Office, where they had been deposited. Fortunately, transcripts for a significant portion of County Cork had been made before 1922.

In 1901-02, Rev. Bartholomew O'Keeffe DD (1856-1927), a priest of the Diocese of Cloyne, made a careful and accurate transcription of the 1766 census for the Diocese of Cloyne. A copy of Fr O'Keeffe's transcript is in the National Archives. Cork County Library also has a copy and the census is reproduced in *O'Kief*, Vol. 8. Of the 56 parishes or unions of parishes in Cloyne in 1766, 48 made returns that named the head of household. The majority of the returns, however, do not provide the townland of residence. There were no returns at all for four parishes, viz., Fermoy, Ballyvourney, Donoughmore and Killeagh. A facsimile reprint of Fr O'Keeffe's transcript of the 1766 Cloyne census is scheduled for publication by Canon B. Troy PP of Midleton in 1998.

Four returns from the 1766 census survive for the parishes in the Diocese of Cork and Ross, viz., Dunbulloge, Kilmichael, Rathbarry and Ringrone. The two former are transcripts made before 1922, the latter two appear to have survived the 1922 fire. The published transcripts for three of these returns are supplemented by valuable annotations regarding secondary surnames and families named in the returns. Sources for the Cork and Ross returns are:

Dunbulloge: Tadhg O'Donnachada, 'Extracts from an Old Census, Parish of Dunbulloge', in JCHAS, 1946, pp. 67-77;

Kilmichael: J. J. Fitzgerald, 'Notes on Names of Inhabitants of Parish of Kilmichael in 1766', in JCHAS, Vol. 26, 1920, pp. 69-79;

Rathbarry: C. J. F. MacCarthy, 'The people of Rathbarry in 1766' in Seanchas Chairbre, No. 3, 1993, pp. 44-51. The original return is in the National Archives, a copy is in Cork County Library;

Ringrone: The original return is in the National Archives; a copy, with supplementary material compiled by C. J. F. MacCarthy, is in Cork County Library.

There are Protestant censuses for 1834 for two Cork parishes. These may have been conducted in response to a government commission on religion and education. That for the parish of Ballymodan which comprised more than half of the town of Bandon, is entitled 'Copies of returns of the parish of Ballymodan, listing the names of the parishioners made… by Rev. A. Knox, 1834' and is in the National Library (NLI Ms. 675); a microfilm copy is in Cork County Library. A detailed description and analysis of this source has been published: Sr Anne McKernan, 'In Search of the Irish Town: rediscovery of a source for Bandon, County Cork', in *Bandon Historical Journal*, No. 2, 1985, pp 23-36. The other 1834 Protestant census is a return of Protestant families in Magourney parish. A copy is deposited with the Magourney Church of Ireland register in the National Archives.

Contemporary with the 1834 censuses, but apparently undated, is a census of the parish of St Mary Shandon, Cork. A statistical analysis of this census was published in 1944, at which time the Ms. census was in the custody of the rector of St Mary Shandon: M. V. Conlon, 'The census of the parish of St Mary Shandon, Cork, c. 1830' in *JCHAS* Vol. 49, 1944, pp 10-18. It would appear to contain approximately 2, 800 names.

Published as an appendix to M. D. Jephson's *Anglo-Irish Miscellany*, Dublin, 1964, are returns of able-bodied Protestants for eight parishes in north-east Cork (Ballyhooly, Brigown, Castletownroche, Clonmeen/Roskeen, Farahy, Glanworth, Kilshannig, Marshalstown). Made for the purpose of raising local militia, the originals are from the Mallow Castle estate records.

Catholic parishes, on occasion, undertook parochial censuses similar to the Church of Ireland censuses discussed above. There are two censuses in existence for the Catholic parish of Midleton; these are dated 1842 and 1848. They are in the custody of Canon B. Troy, PP Midleton, who intends to publish one or both censuses in 1999. In the absence of state census returns for the nineteenth century, religious censuses are a vital historical and genealogical source and it is possible that as research in church archives continues, other parish censuses will come to light.

Chapter 6 Civil Registration

What was Recorded

Civil registration commenced in Ireland on 1 April 1845, with the registration of non-Catholic marriages. From 1 January 1864, registration was extended to all births, deaths and marriages. Births and deaths were to be reported to the local registrar who was to record specified details in a register book. Legislation put the onus on members of the public to report births and deaths. The person reporting the event was officially known as an 'informant'. One of the parents of a new-born child normally reported the birth; in the case of a death, the report would normally be made by a close relative of the deceased.

With the aid of the informant, the registrar recorded the following details on births: date and place of birth; first name; sex; mother's name, surname and maiden name; father's name, address and occupation; date of registration. On deaths, the following details were recorded: date and place of death; name and surname; sex; marital status; age; rank, profession or occupation; cause of death and duration of illness; date of registration.

As well as giving the details of the birth or death, the informant had to give his/her name, address and 'qualification', all of which were recorded in the register. The term 'qualification', as used in a birth or death register, refers to the informant's claim to knowledge of the event. It is usually covered by a phrase such as 'present at birth'. Finally, the informant had to sign the register.

When evaluating information taken from civil registration records, it is always wise to take into consideration who the informant was and the probable extent of his/her knowledge. Information in registers is often quite inaccurate. An informant, when registering a death, for example, had to give the age of the deceased. Research has clearly shown that many informants made wild guesses. It is not unusual for reported ages at death to be up to twenty years in error.

Though it was the duty of a newly married couple to ensure that their marriage was registered, in practice, the officiating clergyman took care of those details. Catholic priests got the newly married couple to sign a Catholic parish register of marriages. Later, he passed the details on to the local registrar who then took care of civil registration. In the case of church marriage ceremonies performed in other Christian Churches, the officiating clergyman acted in a dual capacity. He got the couple to sign both a church register and, in his capacity as a registrar, to sign a civil register also. Registry office marriages, clearly, involved the signing of a civil register of marriages only.

Marriage registers recorded information under the following headings: date of marriage; names of the couple; their ages, marital status, rank or profession; their residence at the time of marriage; the names and occupations of their fathers.

The Administration of Civil Registration

The poor law union was the administrative unit used for civil registration. In 1864 there were 163 such divisions in Ireland; Cork had eighteen three of which extended over the borders of adjacent counties (the Mitchelstown union included portions of Limerick and Tipperary, the Youghal union included part of County Waterford, and the Charleville area was in the Kilmallock, County Limerick union). Each union was further subdivided into dispensary districts. A registrar was appointed to each dispensary district and a superintendent-registrar was appointed to each union. Each time a registrar filled a book, he sent it to his superintendent registrar. Every quarter, he also had to send on certified copies of the registers he had in hand.

The superintendent registrar of a union was to retain the original registers, to index them, and to allow persons to search them on payment of a fee. He also had to send certified copies to the Registrar-General — the official in Dublin in overall charge of registration. The Registrar-General had responsibility for preparing alphabetical indexes of births, deaths and marriages on a countrywide basis for each year.

Apart from a tendency towards greater centralisation, the system has changed little since its commencement. In County Cork, the original registers are now held in three locations — Cork, Mallow and Skibbereen, instead of the original 18 poor law unions. The records of the Registrar-General are kept at Joyce House, Dublin.

There are, therefore, two full sets of birth, death and marriage registers. One set, consisting of copies of the original registers, is stored centrally at Joyce House, Dublin. The original registers, which comprise the other set, are stored at the relevant superintendent registrars' offices throughout the country.

From the researcher's point of view there are some important differences between the locally held records and those held centrally. Superintendent registrars had to have each individual register book indexed, whereas the Registrar-General had to oversee the production of three annual, alphabetical indexes: one for births, one for deaths and one for marriages. A researcher who goes to the central office in Joyce House is permitted to examine the indexes to the records only and not the records themselves. Researchers who go along to the provincial offices may be allowed to examine the original register books.

Whether to do research at local level or centrally depends on the information you have. If you are unable to establish the name of the registrar's district in which a birth, death or marriage took place, then the name and year indexes in Joyce House are your only option. However, once you know the name of the district, the local office will be found to be more productive. Initial research may be carried out in Joyce House and, once the name of the district has been established, the research may be continued locally.

Researching: Dublin

The General Register Office (GRO) is the central repository for records relating to births, deaths and marriages in the Republic of Ireland. The main functions of the office are to provide an efficient registration service, and to meet applications from the public for certificates of births, deaths and marriages for whatever purpose they may be required. The GRO does not undertake genealogical research. However, it does provide excellent facilities for those engaged in such work. The office is very accessible in that it is located centrally. Though the research room is on the first floor, physically handicapped people are facilitated by the provision of a lift and ramps. A public phone and public toilets are also provided in the building, both of which are much appreciated by those engaged in a long day's research. A member of the GRO staff is on duty in the research room and will give assistance to researchers.

When you go along to the GRO you have the option of going to the research room and examining the indexes or going directly to the counter for a birth, death or marriage certificate. Your choice depends on the amount of information you already have.

There are over forty million registered entries on record at the GRO. Anybody looking for a particular entry, therefore, must provide sufficient information to enable a member of the staff to locate and identify that entry. Normally, the following information is required: births — full name, date of birth, exact place of birth, maiden surname of mother, full name of father; deaths— full name, date of death, exact place of death; marriages — full names of both parties including bride's maiden surname, date of marriage, exact place of marriage. If you do not know the exact date of the event, the staff will normally search a range of three years for you. Applications are dealt with while you wait. You can get on the spot service for up to five certificate applications. A full certificate of birth, death or marriage costs IR£5.50.

If you are engaged in genealogical research you are unlikely to have sufficient information to enable the GRO staff to find the birth, death or marriage entry you require. If you are looking for a death entry, for example, you may know the full name of the deceased, the probable place of death and the approximate date. This is where the indexes come in.

These annual compilations list entries in alphabetical order on the basis of surname and first name. Each entry gives the name and surname, the name of the registration district, the page and the number of the volume in which the entry may be found. The indexes to deaths, in addition, give the reported age at death. The indexes to marriages list the husband and wife individually; the wife under her maiden name. The father's name is taken as the surname of the baby in the indexes to births, except in the case of an illegitimate birth in which case the baby takes the mother's surname. From the year 1903 onwards, the mother's maiden name is included in the information given in the indexes to births. This is a useful aid to identification.

The fee payable for permission to search the indexes depends on whether you wish to carry out a 'particular search' or a 'general search'. A particular search involves searching for any one item over a five year period. In other words, the particular search fee of IR£1.50 entitles you to look at five annual indexes of births or deaths or marriages. The general search fee of IR£12.00 entitles the applicant to search through the indexes to either births or deaths during any number of successive hours up to six, or to search the indexes to marriages during any number of successive days not exceeding six. The object of the search need not be specified in the case of a general search.

When you have located what appears to be the entry you are looking for, you can get a photocopy of that item from the copy-register book by giving the name of the registration district, the page number and volume number which you have located in the index to the member of staff on duty in the research room. The photocopy will be provided while you wait and costs IR£1.50.

Late entries are written in at the back of the index books. Another important factor to remember is that some of the indexes to births, deaths and marriages consist of a single index covering the entire year; others consist of four indexes, bound in a single volume, each covering a three-month period of the year. It is important to be aware of this fact as it is quite possible to believe that you have researched a full year when you have, in reality, researched three months only. The following table indicates whether the indexes are yearly or quarterly.

Births Indexes		**Death Indexes**	
1864-1877	Yearly	1864-1877	Yearly
1878-1902	Quarterly	1878-1965	Quarterly
1903-1927	Yearly	1966-to date	Yearly
1928-1932	Quarterly		
1933	Yearly		
1934-1965	Quarterly	**Marriage Indexes**	
1966-to date	Yearly	1845-1877	Yearly
		1878-1965	Quarterly
		1966-to date	Yearly

Researching: Cork

Each of the 26 counties of the Republic has at least one superintendent registrar's Office. Most counties have only one; Donegal, Limerick, Tipperary and Waterford have two each. Cork has three. Each of these offices retains the original records dealing with the county or part of the county under its jurisdiction. These offices are under the control of the relevant regional health board.

As far as access to registers held in county-based superintendent registrars' offices is concerned, there is no consistency. Under the original act, the superintendent registrar was to have the registers indexed and to allow members of the public to search such indexes for a fee. The act makes no reference to whether or not the public could examine the actual registers. But, since the indexes are attached to the registers in most cases, access to the index means access to the registers. Some offices are too small to accommodate researchers and may also have very restricted opening hours. These factors further complicate the situation. Under these circumstances, superintendent registrars must, in large measure, make their own rules and the rules may change with a change in personnel.

Cork City

The superintendent registrar's office in Cork City covers the city and a wide area of the county. The office is normally quite busy but it provides limited research facilities. The charge for spending up to one day — from 10.00 am to 4.00 pm — researching the original register books and their indexes is £6.00. Since only one person can be catered for on any one day, it is necessary to book your day in advance. You can expect to have to wait up to six weeks during the summer months when tourists put extra pressure on resources. During other periods a three to four week waiting period is normal. The registers from the following poor law union districts are to be found at the Cork office (the bracketed numbers refer to the number of registrar's districts): Bandon (5), Cork (14 rural and 7 urban), Kinsale (5), Macroom (5), Midleton (6), Youghal (2).

Mallow

The superintendent registrar's office for North Cork is situated in the County Council offices in Mallow. It is open three afternoons per week, Monday, Wednesday and Friday from 2.00 pm to 3.30 pm. These opening times are for the purposes of transacting the normal business of the office — the issuing of certificates and the registration of births, deaths and marriages. Appointments may be made, at the discretion of the superintendent registrar, for researchers to personally examine the register books at periods outside those times but within the opening hours of the County Council office, that is Monday to Friday from 9.00 am to 5.00 pm. The office is not too busy and an appointment can usually be arranged without very much prior notice. A fee of £6.00 is payable for this service. The office holds registers for the following poor law union areas (again, in brackets after each poor law union is the number of registrar's districts in the area): Fermoy (5), Kanturk (4), Mallow (6), Millstreet (2), Mitchelstown (2). The Charleville/Rathluirc area of the county originally formed part of the Kilmallock, County Limerick poor law union. It constituted one registrar's district. The registers for the area are also in the Mallow office.

Skibbereen

The Skibbereen office covers six poor law unions with a total of eighteen registrars' districts in West Cork (numbers in bracket refer to the number of registrar's districts in each union): Bantry (4), Castletown (2), Clonakilty (3), Dunmanway (3), Skibbereen (4), Skull (2). The office has very restricted opening times: Monday and Thursday from 10.00 am to 12.30 pm. Over the years, the superintendent registrar Seamus Ryan has been very helpful to family history enthusiasts. At no charge and in his own time he has often gone back to the office in the evening and gone through the registers with researchers who have phoned up and made appointments.

Undoubtedly, research at the local offices is more interesting and more satisfactory than researching in Joyce House in Dublin. One great advantage is that you are handling the original registers, so you are likely to find entries which have been signed by your ancestors as informants of births or deaths. In the case of many of our ancestors, such a signature may be the only thing they left after them that still survives. An even greater advantage of researching locally is that, having found one child of a family, it is quite easy to locate others as they are likely to have been registered in the same registrar's district, and so their entries should be in the same register book or to be in earlier or later ones in the series. Birth entries may lead to marriage and death entries. Much family history material may be acquired with little effort. However, unless you can pinpoint fairly accurately the place of residence of the person you are researching, you cannot make any progress in a superintendent registrar's office.

Unlike Joyce House, where you must search yearly indexes, date is less important than place at a superintendent registrars' offices. This is because in these local offices the register books are arranged on the basis of registrars' districts, that is the geographical areas which they cover.

Some of these districts are unchanged since they were originally set up in 1864, especially the rural ones and the office personnel should have no difficulty in finding the appropriate registers. But civil registration, it must be remembered, is still ongoing and various amalgamations have taken place over the long period during which the system has operated, especially in Cork City and there may be some difficulties where this is the case.

Chapter 7 Griffith's Valuation

In Chapter 4, Administrative Divisions, reference is made to the setting up of a workhouse system in Ireland in 1838 for the relief of the poor. The country was divided up into 163 new administrative units called poor law unions. Each union was to consist of a market town and the countryside within a radius of about fifteen miles. A workhouse was to be built in the town and the destitute within the union could apply for admission. No outdoor relief was on offer. It was all or nothing.

Each poor law union was administered by a board of guardians who were elected by all property holders within the union. These electors had to pay for the upkeep of the workhouse and its occupants. An effort was made to ensure that this local tax was in proportion to the means of those levied. For this reason it was found necessary to ascertain the value of the property held by each householder in every union. Sir Richard Griffith was the official who managed this huge property valuation, so the Primary Valuation of Tenements, to give it its official title, is generally known as Griffith's *Valuation*.

The Primary Valuation of Tenements

Griffith's valuers examined every dwelling house and outhouse, every field and garden in Ireland. Nothing was too small, too insignificant or too remote to escape their attentions. The purpose of their examinations was to put a monetary value on every piece of property and to ascertain who was in possession of it and from whom it was rented. The value they put on the various properties was not the market value, but the amount of profit that the occupier could reasonably be expected to make from it in the course of one year.

When the valuation had been completed, every householder in a poor law union had a rateable valuation on his property, and the board of guardians of every union knew what was the total valuation of all the property in their union. The board then estimated how much it would cost to run the workhouse for the year and struck a rate by dividing that sum by the total valuation of the union. In the early years of this system, a small farmer might have had his property valued at about £5; the poor law union rate might be something like three pence in the pound. His annual tax liability would then be fifteen pence, that is 1s 3d in the currency of that time.

Field, House and Tenure Books

All this is of interest to genealogists because of the documents the valuation generated. Most of this material has survived and is quite accessible to researchers. In their initial survey, the valuers took notes on three aspects of the holdings they examined — the quality of the soil, details of the buildings, and the title of the occupier to the property. Separate notebooks were used to record the three types of data: Field Books, House Books and Tenure Books. All the notebooks are laid out in tabular form, each one requiring the name of the occupier to be written in, plus other kinds of information under the various headings.

Field books are of least interest as far as family history research is concerned, since they focus on the quality and productivity of the soil. House books are of more interest. They give detailed descriptions of not only dwelling houses — down to the smallest — but also all of the barns, stables, sheds and outhouses that may have formed part of the holding. The descriptions are so detailed and the measurements so precise that it would be possible to reconstruct an outline of what they looked like. The tenure books are the most important of all. Under the heading 'Tenure and Year Let' may be found a description of the conditions under which the property was held — for example whether the occupiers held a lease or were 'tenants-at-will' who paid an annual rent but had no guarantee of longer possession. The date when the occupiers first came into possession of the property is a very useful piece of information which may not be so easily available elsewhere. Sometimes, in the case of leaseholders, information is given about the duration of the lease.

These notebooks are held in the National Archives. They are arranged by county, barony, parish and townland. Indexes in the reading room give the call numbers of these notebooks, so there is little difficulty in accessing them.

The Published Valuation

When the information had been gathered up by the valuers, it was set down in tabular form, standard for the whole country, and published. The 200 volumes cover the country, county by county. The publication dates for the Cork volumes range from 1851 to 1853. Each townland appears in alphabetical order within its civil parish, the civil parishes are arranged alphabetically within their baronies. There are eight columns in Griffith's *Valuation*. Map references are listed in the first column. They are keyed to Ordnance Survey maps held by the valuers on which each holding was marked out. The names of the occupiers appear in column two, and in column three are the names of the 'immediate lessors'. They were usually, but not always, the landlords. Sometimes a farmer would sublet some of his holding to, perhaps, a labourer. In that case the labourer would appear as the occupier and the farmer as the 'immediate lessor'. A description of the 'tenement' or holding followed. The most common description is 'house, offices and land', the offices referring to farm buildings. The final four columns are taken up by figures: the area of the land in acres, roods and perches; the valuation of the land; the valuation of the buildings; and the total valuation.

The information in the published version of Griffith's *Valuation* frequently differs slightly from that found in the earlier notebooks, indicating that some revisions had been made. If an occupier died shortly after the initial survey and was replaced by someone else, the name of the former would appear in the notebooks and the name of the latter would appear in the published valuation. Since any such replacement was likely to be related to the original occupier — a son or a wife — many researchers are lucky enough to find two generations of a family in this way.

Griffith's *Valuation* is to be found in the National Library, the National Archives and in many other libraries and archives both in hard copy and in microfiche.

Valuation Maps

The maps referred to earlier are very useful because both the holdings and the houses are marked out clearly. These maps can enable a researcher to pinpoint exactly where an ancestor's farm and house were situated in the 1850s. Later, when visiting the ancestral place, the site of the house can be found even though the building itself may be long gone. Up to recently, it was possible to get a photocopy of the maps by calling or writing to the Valuation Office. The maps have deteriorated over time and are now considered to be in too fragile a condition for such copying. Recently they were moved to the National Archives. The Valuation Office retains scans of the maps which may be examined on computer screen. Printouts of the maps are available at the Valuation Office but are expensive. A full map costs in the region of IR£60. However, the sections of interest may be purchased for less, the price depending on the size of the map required.

Indexes to Griffith's *Valuation*

There are several ways of locating an individual in Griffith's *Valuation*. If you know the townland in which he lived, it is simply a matter of using the *Townland Index* to find the civil parish and barony in which that townland is located and then getting the appropriate volume or microfiche of Griffith's *Valuation*. If you know the ancestor's name but not the townland, there are several indexes to help you.

The oldest is the National Library's 'Householders Index'. It was produced in typescript form and never published as a book. Photocopies of it have been made and it is widely available in libraries and archives in Dublin and beyond. This index is not as simple and straightforward as such works are expected to be. First of all, it covers both Griffith's *Valuation* and another source — the tithe applotment books — which will be dealt with in the next chapter. There is a volume for each county. The volume for Cork consists, first of all, of an alphabetical list of all the surnames that appear in either of those two sources for the county. After each name the letter 'G' or the letter 'T' appears, or both 'G' and 'T'. The former, standing for 'Griffith's *Valuation*', indicates that the name appears in that source, the latter standing for 'the tithe applotment books', indicates that that surname is present in the tithe applotment books. The name of the barony in which the surname appears is given after each surname entry. There is a similar index for each barony in the typescript, reference to which allows you to narrow down the location of the surname to a parish or parishes within the barony. After that, you must go the Griffith's *Valuation* and search all townlands in the parish to find the actual surname entry. First names or titles do not appear in the index, only surnames. It is not possible, therefore, to eliminate entries without actually checking them out in the valuation. Unless the surname you are researching is fairly rare, the 'Householders Index' is of little value. The index gives good guidance as to how rare a surname is, in that the number of times the name appears in a barony or parish is given in each entry — the number appears after the letter 'G'. For example the entry 'Richardson G3 T Carrigrohane' means that the surname Richardson appears three times in Griffith's Valuation in the parish of Carrigrohane and appears at least once in the tithe applotment books of the same parish.

The second index, published in microfiche form by All-Ireland Heritage Inc, is much easier to manage. It consists of one alphabetical run of surnames for the whole county. First names and titles are also included. Each entry gives not only the name of the townland and parish in which the name appears, but also the page number of Griffith's *Valuation* on which the name may be found. Occupiers of land who were not householders are not included in the list. This avoids unnecessary and confusing duplication. People who held patches of land in several townlands appear in the valuation several times. They appear in the index only once — in the townland in which they are credited with holding a dwelling house.

The third and most recent index takes advantage of modern technology. It is a CD-Rom index produced by Irish World of County Tyrone and the Genealogical Publishing Company of Baltimore, USA. This index gives the full name of the householder, his county, parish and townland of residence, with a reference also to the microfiche version of the valuation on which the index is based. This huge undertaking was completed after three years of work and the assistance of 100 members of the staff of Irish World.

Soon to come on the market is the whole of Griffith's *Valuation* on a set of five CD-Rom discs, including an index. The set is currently priced at IR£1,500. The publishers of this package are European Micropublishing Services of Dublin.

The Cancelled Books

Griffith's *Valuation* was compiled for the purposes of collecting local taxes. The published version of the valuation lists the people who were liable for those taxes at the time of publication. As time passed by, the occupiers of houses and lands changed, due to death, emigration and the like. New people took their places and became liable for the taxes for a while, until they too were replaced. The authorities kept careful records of all of these changes. Manuscript copies of the original valuation were held and continuously updated. When a property holder died and was replaced by someone else, a line was drawn through the original holder's name and the name of the new occupier was written above it. The date of the change was also noted. The changes were made in inks of various colours. A name change and a date in the same colour indicated that that particular change took place in that year. In time, these record books had so many changes noted in them that, despite the colour-coding, they became difficult to interpret. At that point, the most up to date information was transcribed into a new record book and the whole procedure began all over again.

Taken together, these 'cancelled books' as they are called, provide a history of every property holding in Ireland. It is possible to follow the chain of possession from the date of the original valuation right up to the present time. The dates when the changes of possession took place can be very useful to the family historian. Often, the change from father to son or husband to wife is an indication of a death of the previous occupier. If the surname changes, it could indicate a marriage or point to the emigration of the earlier occupiers.

All the old record books were retained and are available to researchers at the Valuation Office, Dublin. It is possible to get photocopies of the pages of the cancelled books that are relevant to your research. However, considering the use of colour already mentioned, the full picture may not come across in a photocopy.

Chapter 8   Tithe Applotment Books

The tithe was one tenth of the produce of the land payable in kind to the church. At first it was a voluntary donation, but later it became a compulsory levy in most countries. The tithe was a particularly contentious tax in Ireland in the early nineteenth century. Only about ten percent of the population belonged to the Church of Ireland, which was the official established church, yet the members of all other churches had to pay tithes for its upkeep.

Background

When Daniel O'Connell's Catholic Emancipation campaign was coming to a successful conclusion he tried to keep the resentment against the tithe under control. He did not want violent incidents to damage the prospects of getting equal rights for Catholics from the British government. When the tithe continued to be demanded even after the granting of Emancipation in 1829, many people were bitterly disappointed and the so called tithe war started.

A very determined refusal to pay tithes began in Leinster in 1830 and spread quickly throughout the country. In several areas there were violent incidents resulting in injury and death. These conflicts were often started when the local Church of Ireland clergyman demanded tithe payment from the local Catholic priest, was refused and then seized some of the priest's property, as was his right under the law.

The refusal to pay the tithe reduced many of the parochial clergy of the Established Church to a state of near destitution. The government introduced a number of initiatives to remedy the situation. In 1832 they brought in a compensation scheme for those worst hit. A fund of £60,000 was made available to those who could show that, having made a serious effort to collect the sums due to them in 1831, the money remained unpaid. The government used the army in a bloody campaign to collect the outstanding debts. Only one percent of the total was collected and the campaign cost twice as much as it actually brought in.

A compromise was reached in 1838 when it was agreed that the tithe would be reduced by 25 percent and be payable as part of the rent. The landlord rather than the tenant had the responsibility of paying the tithe from that point. The tithe was finally abolished in 1869.

The conversion of the tithe from a payment in produce to a money payment, known as tithe commutation, was an important part of the process of making the tithe more palatable. In 1823 an act was passed allowing for voluntary commutation. Under this act, two valuers were appointed to each civil parish, one by the ratepayers and the other by the Established Church. Their function was to put a monetary value on the tithe for each holding. This could be done by agreement or by a valuation process which took into account the quality of the land and the average price of grain in the previous seven years. An act of 1832 made tithe commutation compulsory. Under this act, a single commissioner was appointed by the Lord Lieutenant to each civil parish, to put a tithe value on all the holdings in the parish.

Tithe Applotment Books for Cork

The valuers' notebooks are known as tithe applotments books and they are extant for almost all of the civil parishes in Cork. About two thirds of Cork civil parishes were valued under the 1823 act. Some parishes appear to have been valued twice as there are two tithe applotment books for about thirty Cork civil parishes. See Table 1, pages 25-30 for a listing of the dates of the tithe applotment books for the various civil parishes in County Cork.

Tithe applotment books, unlike Griffith's *Valuation,* are not uniform in appearance or content. Generally, pages are divided into several columns. The names of the occupiers of each townland are listed in the first column, followed by columns listing the area and valuation of the occupier's holding and the tithe payable. These documents are in the National Archives. Not every householder appears in the tithe applotment books.

Tithe Defaulters Lists

As already mentioned, a compensation scheme for clergy who were badly hit by the tithe war was introduced in 1832. An application for relief had to be accompanied by a statement outlining in detail the amount of tithes which were due to the applicant and the efforts he had made to collect them. He also had to send a complete list of 'tithe defaulters' in the parish, giving in each case the address, amount of tithe due and other details. Standardised printed forms called 'schedules' were made available to applicants, the blank parts of which were filled by the clergyman.

Tithe defaulters lists exist for eleven Cork civil parishes: Ballymoney, Ballyvourney, Clondrohid, Clonpriest, Creagh, Drishane, Ightermurragh, Kildorrery, Killeagh, St Nathlash and Wallstown. They are available at the National Archives (call numbers: OPMA 156/2/51-60). Even though there may be only a few years' difference between the date of the tithe applotment book of a parish and the that of the tithe defaulters list, many changes may have taken place during the intervening years. A comparison between the tithe applotment book for the parish of Ballyvourney, dated 18 December 1827, and the defaulters list for the same parish, dated 5 July 1832, some four and a half years later, indicates how much may be gleaned from this additional source. The most striking feature of the defaulters list, when compared to the earlier complete list of people required to pay tithes is that there are more names on the defaulters list than the tithe applotment book; 312 compared to 298. Clearly, virtually nobody paid tithes in 1831. Out of a total of £500 due to the rector, less than £17 was collected.

The lapse of time is reflected in the second list in a number of ways. Thirty-five changes in surname occur, indicating that a significant number of the earlier occupiers had been replaced. Eleven changes in first name occur, showing that another member of the same family was now the proprietor, possibly a son replacing his father. Over twenty women are listed without first name in the applotment book, the term 'Widow' being used instead, e.g. 'Widow Kelly'. In the defaulters list, the first name is also included, e.g. 'Widow Mary Kelly. The passage of time had resulted in six more proprietors being listed as widows. In all, there are 80 significant changes between the tithe applotment book and the defaulters list. In some defaulters lists the occupations of those listed are given. This is not so in the case of the Ballyvourney list, possibly because the parish was populated almost exclusively by farmers.

Page from Catholic Marriage register of St. Finbar's, South parish 1810.

Chapter 9   Catholic Parish Records

The Catholic Church kept registers of baptisms and marriages. The value of these records to the genealogist varies. They were kept from an early date in some parishes, particularly in the towns and cities, but generally have a starting date of around 1820. The records are not standardised. The most useful baptismal records give the name of the child, the name and address of the father, maiden name of the mother, names of witnesses and the date. Some give nothing more than the date, name of the child, mother's name — first name only — and the name of the father. Marriage entries, at the minimum, give the date of marriage and the names of the bride, groom and witnesses. Some, in addition, give the addresses of both parties and their fathers' names. Poor handwriting in some registers can make research a very slow process. Catholic parish registers are kept locally by the parish priests. They have been microfilmed and are available in that form at the National Library of Ireland. The Mormon Family History Centres are able to provide these microfilms also. Some have been published in *O'Kief.* All the Catholic parish registers for the diocese of Cloyne have been indexed by the Mallow Heritage Centre which accepts research commissions on a fee basis.

Table 2 lists all Catholic parishes in County Cork in alphabetical order. This list is taken from *Guy's County and City of Cork Directory of 1875-76.* Column two names the diocese in which the parish is situated. This is important because in the case of the diocese of Cloyne, Kerry and Limerick permission of the bishop is required before even microfilm copies of the registers may be examined at the National Library. This permission is given by return of post or fax. If requested, the diocesan authorities will send the permission directly to the National Library.

The third and fourth columns refer to the date runs of baptismal and marriage records available for the parish. In the case of the diocese of Cloyne, the list used is that issued by the Mallow Heritage Centre. In the case of the other dioceses, the information is taken from the microfilm indexes of the National Library of Ireland. The last column gives the modern name of the parish — useful if you wish to contact the parish priest for permission to examine the records. The original records of each parish are retained by the parish priest. The name and postal address of each parish priest will be found in a current edition of the annualy-published Irish Catholic Directory, which is available in most reference libraries, or in the annual directories produced by the dioceses.

Catholic boundaries were subject to change from time to time. Canon B. Troy, writing about the Catholic parishes in the diocese of Cloyne, says that very few of them did not change. He refers to many changes that would be quite significant from the point of view of the genealogist, for example: 'the seven townlands of Clonmeen which were north of the Blackwater became part of Castlemagner parish'; and 'Rockchapel and Meelin became an independent parish in 1866.

Rockchapel and Meelin records up to then would be in the Newmarket Registers.'
Some of these changes are mentioned in the table under 'Notes'.

Table 2: Catholic Parishes of Cork

Catholic Parish	Diocese	Baptisms	Marriages	Source	Notes
Adrigole *see* Kilcaskan S.					
Aghabullogue *see* Coachford					
Aghada	Cloyne	1792-1893	1785-1895	MHC	
Aghadown	Ross	1822-1880	1822-1865	NLI	now Aughadown
Aghinagh	Cloyne	1848-1895	1848-1895	MHC	
Allihies *see* Kilnamanagh					
Anakissy	Cloyne	1805-1895	1805-1895	MHC	now Killavullen
Ardfield	Ross	1801-1876	1800-1880	NLI	now Ardfield & Rathbarry
Ballinamona *see* Mourne Abbey					
Ballincollig	Cork	1828-1880	1828-1880	NLI	
Ballindangan *see* Glanworth					
Ballinhassig	Cork	1821-1880	1821-1880	NLI	
Ballyclogh	Cloyne	1807-1896	1805-1896	MHC	now Ballyclough
Ballygran	Limerick	1841-1880	1841-1880	NLI	
Ballyhay	Cloyne	1807-1899	1811-1899	MHC	now Ballyhea
Ballymacoda	Cloyne	1835-1899	1835-1899	MHC	now B.macoda &Ladysbridge
Ballyvourney	Cloyne	1810-1895	1871-1895	MHC	also in *O'Kief*
Bandon	Cork	1794-1880	1794-1880	NLI	
Banteer *see* Clonmeen					
Bantry	Cork	1788-1880	1788-1880	NLI	
Barryroe	Ross	1804-1873	1771-1873	NLI	
Blackrock	Cork	1810-1880	1810-1880	NLI	created in 1848
Blarney	Cloyne	1791-1895	1791-1895	MHC	
Boherbue *see* Kilmeen					
Bonane & Glengarriff *see* Kilcaskan					
Buttevant	Cloyne	1814-1895	1814-1896	MHC	
Caheragh	Cork	1818-1880	1818-1880	NLI	
Carrigaline	Cork	1826-1880	1826-1880	NLI	
Carrigtohill	Cloyne	1817-1899	1817-1899	MHC	now Carrigtwohill
Castlehaven	Ross	1742-1880		NLI	
Castlelyons	Cloyne	1790-1896	1830-1896	MHC	
Castlemagner	Cloyne	1832-1899	1832-1899	MHC	
Castlemartyr *see* Imogeela					
Castletownbere *see* Kilaconenagh					
Castletownroche	Cloyne	1811-1899	1829-1899	MHC	
Charleville	Cloyne	1827-1895	1774-1895	MHC	
Churchtown *see* Liscarroll					
Clonakilty	Ross	1809-1873	1811-1880	NLI	now Clonakilty & Darrara
Clondrohid	Cloyne	1807-1895	1807-1895	MHC	
Clonmeen	Cloyne	1828-1899	1828-1899	MHC	now Banteer
Clontade & Ballymartle	Cork	1836-1880	1836-1880	NLI	now Clontead, created 1860
Cloyne	Cloyne	1791-1880	1786-1880	NLI	
Coachford	Cloyne	1820-1895	1820-1895	MHC	now Aghabullogue

Catholic Parish	Diocese	Baptisms	Marriages	Source	Notes
Cobh *see* Queenstown					
Conna	Cloyne	1834-1895	1834-1895	MHC	
Courceys	Cork	1819-1880	1819-1880	NLI	
Desert & Enniskeane	Cork	1813-1880	1819-1880	NLI	now E.keane & Desertserges
Doneraile	Cloyne	1815-1895	1815-1895	MHC	
Donoughmore	Cloyne	1790-1899	1790-1899	MHC	
Douglas	Cork	1812-1880	1812-1880	NLI	
Drimoleague	Cork	1817-1880	1817-1880	NLI	
Drishane	Kerry	1853-1880	1855-1880	NLI	now Millstreet, also in *O'Kief*
Dromtarriff	Kerry	1832-1880	1832-1880	NLI	also in *O'Kief*
Dunmanway	Cork	1818-1880	1818-1880	NLI	
Enniskeane *see* Desert & Enniskeane					
Eyeries see Kilcatherine					
Fermoy	Cloyne	1828-1899	1828-1899	MHC	
Freemount	Cloyne	1827-1895	1827-1896	MHC	
Glanmire	Cork	1806-1841	1803-1880	NLI	includes Carrignavar
Glantane	Cloyne	1829-1895	1858-1895	MHC	
Glanworth	Cloyne	1836-1899	1836-1899	MHC	now G.worth & Ballindangan
Glengarriff *see* Kilcaskan					
Glounthane	Cork	1864-1880	1864-1880	NLI	now Glounthaune
Grenagh	Cloyne	1840-1899	1840-1899	MHC	
Imogeela	Cloyne	1833-1895	1833-1895	MHC	now Castlemartyr
Inchigeela *see* Iveleary					
Inniscarra	Cloyne	1814-1895	1814-1899	MHC	
Innishannon	Cork	1825-1880	1834-1880	NLI	
Iveleary	Cork	1816-1880	1816-1880	NLI	now Uibh Laoire, in *O'Kief*
Kanturk	Cloyne	1822-1899	1824-1899	MHC	
Kilaconenagh	Kerry	1819-1878	1819-1880	NLI	now Castletownbere
Kilbrittain	Cork	1810-1880	1810-1880	NLI	
Kilcaskan	Kerry	1846-1880	1846-1880	NLI	now Bonane & Glengarriff
Kilcaskan S.	Kerry	1830-1880	1830-1880	NLI	now Adrigole
Kilcatherine	Kerry	1843-1880	1824-1880	NLI	now Eyeries
Kildorrery	Cloyne	1824-1895	1824-1895	MHC	
Killavullen *see* Annakissy					
Killeagh	Cloyne	1829-1895	1829-1895	MHC	
Kilmacabea	Ross	1832-1880	1832-1880	NLI	now Kilmacbea
Kilmallock	Limerick	1837-1880	1837-1880	NLI	
Kilmeen	Kerry	1833-1880	1843-1880	NLI	now Boherbue, also in *O'Kief*
Kilmeen	Ross	1821-1880		NLI	now Kilmeen & Castleventry
Kilmichael	Cork	1819-1880	1819-1880	NLI	
Kilmurry	Cork	1786-1880	1786-1880	NLI	
Kilnamanagh	Kerry	1822-1880	1822-1880	NLI	now Allihies
Kilnamartery	Cloyne	1803-1894	1803-1895	MHC	now Kilnamartyra
Kilworth	Cloyne	1829-1899	1829-1899	MHC	
Kinalea *see* Tracton					
Kinsale	Cork	1805-1880	1828-1880	NLI	
Liscarroll	Cloyne	1812-1895	1813-1895	MHC	
Lisgoold	Cloyne	1807-1899	1821-1899	MHC	
Lismore	Waterford & Lismore	1820-1880	1822-1880	NLI	

Catholic Parish	Diocese	Baptisms	Marriages	Source	Notes
Macroom	Cloyne	1803-1899	1780-1898	MHC	some records in *O'Kief*
Mallow	Cloyne	1809-1899	1757-1899	MHC	
Meelin	Cloyne	1865-1899	1865-1899	MHC	now Rockchapel & Meelin
Midleton	Cloyne	1819-1899	1819-1899	MHC	
Milford *see* Freemount					
Millstreet *see* Drishane					
Mitchelstown	Cloyne	1792-1899	1780-1898	MHC	
Monkstown	Cork	1875-1880	1875-1880	NLI	Created in 1875
Mournabbey	Cloyne	1830-1899	1830-1899	MHC	now Mourne Abbey
Muinteravara	Cork	1820-1880	1819-1880	NLI	now Muintir Bháire
Murragh & Kinneigh	Cork	1834-1864	1834-1880	NLI	now Murragh & Templemartin
Newmarket	Cloyne	1833-1899	1833-1899	MHC	
Ovens	Cork	1816-1877	1816-1877	NLI	
Passage West	Cork	1795-1880	1795-1880	NLI	
Queenstown	Cloyne	1812-1899	1812-1899	MHC	now Cobh
Rath and the Islands	Ross	1818-1880	1819-1880	NLI	
Rathcormac	Cloyne	1798-1899	1829-1899	MHC	
Rockchapel *see* Meelin					
Rosscarbery	Ross	1814-1880	1820-1880	NLI	now Rosscarbery & Lissavaird
St Finbar's (South Parish)	Cork	1789-1880	1775-1880	NLI	now St Finbarr's South
St Mary's (N.Cathedral)	Cork	1748-1880	1748-1880	NLI	now Cathedral of St Mary & St Anne
St Patrick's	Cork	1831-1880	1832-1880	NLI	created in 1848
St Peter and Paul's	Cork	1766-1880	1776-1880	NLI	
Shandrum	Cloyne	1829-1895	1829-1895	MHC	
Skibbereen	Ross	1814-1880	1837-1880	NLI	
Skull (East)	Cork	1807-1880	1809-1880	NLI	now Schull
Skull (West)	Cork	1827-1880	1827-1880	NLI	now Goleen
Timoleague	Ross	1842-1880	1771-1880	NLI	now Timoleague & Clogagh
Tracton	Cork	1802-1880	1840-1880	NLI	now Tracton Abbey
Watergrasshill	Cork	1836-1880		NLI	
Youghal	Cloyne	1803-1899	1801-1899	MHC	

Chapter 10 Church of Ireland Parish Records

In content, Church of Ireland baptismal and marriage registers are essentially the same as those of the Catholic Church which have been dealt with already. Additionally, most Church of Ireland parishes kept burial registers.

Up to about 1830, plain paper registers were generally used. These registers tended to be 'mixed', in that one book served to record baptismal, marriage and burial information. From 1830 to 1845, printed, mixed registers came into use. In 1845, duplicate marriage registers were introduced as non-Catholic marriages became registerable under legislation. Around 1905, new duplicate books became necessary to accommodate new categories of information. When a new type of register was introduced, the old ones were then discontinued, even though in some cases only a few pages may have been used. This accounts for the large number of registers held by some parishes despite their having a small Church of Ireland population.

After the disestablishment of the Church of Ireland in 1869 — when it ceased to be the official state church — most of its records, including parish registers, became public records. Legislation already enacted required that the Church's baptismal and burial registers up to 1870 and marriage records up to 1845 to be deposited in the Public Record Office. However, this was later amended to allow the Church of Ireland registers to be retained locally, if desired, provided certain conditions were fulfilled. In 1922 the destruction of those registers that were sent to the Public Record Office for safe-keeping was total. It is important to remember, however, that copies of the Church of Ireland marriage registers from 1845 survived because they were stored in the General Register Office, where they are still available to researchers (see Chapter 6).

Surviving Church of Ireland parish registers are either held locally or at the Representative Church Body Library(RCB), Dublin. Generally speaking, marriage registers up to 1845 and baptism and burial registers up to 1870 have been filmed by the National Archives and copies are held by the National Archives, the RCB, and Cobh Heritage Project.

Table 3 lists all the Church of Ireland parishes in County Cork as they were in 1863. This list is taken from *Charles' Irish Church Directory* for that year. As explained earlier, parish boundaries often changed, and it can be difficult to ascertain which parish an ancestor lived in. *Church and Parish Records of the United Diocese of Cork, Cloyne, and Ross* by Rev. J. H. Cole is a very useful tool for following the various changes that took place in the Church of Ireland parish structure between 1863 and 1903. However, it may not be necessary to get too involved in tracing the histories of individual parishes because when a parish became part of a union it was the practice to continue using the original parish registers so long as the original parish church continued to be used.

Column two lists the diocese in which the parish was situated. Columns three, four and five give the date runs of the baptismal, marriage and death registers respectively of each parish, when they are known to exist. Five lists were consulted for this information. First of all, the list produced by the Representative Church Body Library, *RCB* entitled: 'A Handlist of Church of Ireland Parish Registers in the Representative Church Body Library, Dublin'. The RCB is principal repository for the parish records of the Church in the Republic of Ireland. The second list used is that produced by the Mallow Heritage Centre *MHC*. This is the Irish Genealogical Project indexing centre for North Cork. That list, as well as giving date runs, also includes the number of items indexed in each set of records. This information, which is bracketed after the date-runs in the table below, may be indicative of the smallness of the Church of Ireland population within the parish or the quantity of records to have survived the Public Record Office fire. The third list is taken from the contents pages of *O'Kief* and designated *O'Kief.* The fourth list is that produced by Michael Leader ML and published in an article entitled: 'Transcripts of County Cork Parish Registers' in *The Irish Genealogist,* Vol. 3, No. 5. The fifth list is from *A Table of Church of Ireland Parochial Records and Copies* edited by Noel Reid. Items from this list are designated NA as they are to be found in microfilm form in the National Archives, Dublin, or *(LC)* — bracketed — when it is indicated that they are in local custody. Local information provided by the Cobh Genealogical Project was also used. Registers indicated by that source to be still in local custody are designated *LC* — without brackets.

Information on the records of many parishes appears in more than one list and the date runs given for the same parish in different lists may vary very significantly. However, to avoid clutter, only one series of dates is included. Researchers are advised, therefore, to check the other lists also, all of which are widely available in libraries. Additional lists are also available, such as the Grove-White Abstracts referred to in John Grenham's *Tracing Your Irish Ancestors,* p. 149.

An approach to the Rector of the union in which the ceremony is thought to have taken place should be considered. Contact details are available from Mr W. Baker, Church of Ireland, Diocesan Office, 14 Cove Street, Cork City; phone (021) 272262. Cobh Genealogical Project (Merville, Cobh, County Cork) is engaged in the very long-term task of computerising the Church of Ireland records for the entire united dioceses of Cork, Cloyne and Ross. Requests to this body should be in writing and give all the information which the enquirer already possesses. If the relevant records have been indexed, they will be searched for a fee of Ir£10.

The final column indicates which list the information regarding the records is taken from. This also points to the location of the records.

Table 3: Church of Ireland Parishes of Cork

Church of Ireland

Parish	Diocese	Baptisms	Marriages	Deaths	Location
Abbeymahon	Ross	1827-1878			RCB, Cork Co. Libr.
Abbeystrewry	Ross	1778-1875	1778-	1778-1875	(LC), NA
Aghabulloge	Cloyne	1808-1877	1808-1843	1809-1879	*O'Kief*
Aghada	Cloyne	1815-1875	1815-1845	1815-1875	(LC), NA

Church of Ireland

Parish	Diocese	Baptisms	Marriages	Deaths	Location
Aghadown	Ross				none
Aglish	Cork				none
Aglishdrinagh	Cloyne				
Ahern	Cloyne	1846-1892 (20)			MHC
Ahinagh	Cloyne				none
Ardagh	Cloyne				none
Ardfield	Ross				
Ardnageehy	Cork				none
Athnowen	Cork				none
Ballinaboy	Cork				none
Ballinadee	Cork				none
Ballyclough	Cloyne	1795-1900	1798-1848	1796-1900	NA
		also marriages	1845-1898 (38) in MHC		
Ballycotton	Cloyne				none
Ballydehob	Cork				chapel of ease Schull
Ballyfeard	Cork				
Ballyhay	Cloyne	1764-1899 (679)	1777-1844 (51)	1777-1898 (712)	MHC
Ballyhooly	Cloyne	1850-1899 (13)			
Ballymartle	Cork	1799-1868		1800-1876	ML
Ballymodan	Cork	1695-1878	1695-1858	1695-1878	RCB
Ballymoney	Cork				
Ballynoe	Cloyne	1882-1899 (9)	1858-1896 (4)	1886-1898 (9)	MHC
Ballyvourney	Cloyne	1845-1935	1845-1935		O'Kief
Berehaven	Ross	1787-1875	1787-1845	1787-1875	(LC), NA
Bohillane	Cloyne				
Bridgetown	Cloyne	1859-1871			ML
Brigown	Cloyne	1768-1899 (652)	1810-1848 (80)	1810-1899 (428)	MHC
Brinny	Cork	1797-1884	1797-1844	1797-1844	RCB
Buttevant	Cloyne	1800-1900 (319)	1845-1899 (259)	1800-1899 (147)	MHC, O'Kief
Caheragh	Cork	1736-1875	1835-1845	1835-1875	(LC), NA
Cannaway	Cork		1845-1872		RCB
Carrigaline	Cork	1724-1756	1726-1792		RCB
Carrigamleary	Cloyne	1848-1871 (4)			MHC, *O'Kief*
Carrigdownane	Cloyne				
Carrigrohane	Cork				none
Carrigrohanebeg	Cloyne				none
Carrigtohill	Cloyne		1848-1955		RCB
Castlehaven	Ross				none
Castlelyons	Cloyne	1838-1840 (343)	1846-1898 (26)	1890 (1)	MHC
Castlemagner	Cloyne		1849-1899 (14)		MHC
Castlemartyr	Cloyne	1800-1900 (46)	1845-1894 (38)		MHC
Castletownroche	Cloyne	1829-1899 (150)	1845-1895 (26)		MHC
Churchtown	Cloyne	1806-1865	1800-1842	1826-1872	ML
Clenore	Cloyne	1814-1876	1814-1840	1829-1855	ML
Clondrohid	Cloyne		1848-1884		RCB, *O'Kief*

Church of Ireland

Parish	Diocese	Baptisms	Marriages	Deaths	Location
Clondullane	Cloyne		1848-1899 (25)		MHC
Clonfert	Cloyne	1845-1847	1845-1847		*O'Kief*
Clonmeen	Cloyne	1889-1892 (2)	1848-1862 (5)	1892 (1)	MHC
Clonmel	Cloyne	1761-1875	1761-1845	1761-1865	(LC)
Clonmult	Cloyne				none
Clonpriest	Cloyne	1851-1870 (6)			MHC
Cloyne	Cloyne	1844-1863			RCB
Cobh *see* Clonmel					
Coole	Cloyne	no records see Castlelyons			
Cooline	Cloyne				
Cork City Parishes Cork					
Christ Church		*see* Holy Trinity			see p. 65
Holy Trinity		1643-1857	1646-1845	1644-1857	RCB, see note p. 63
St Anne's Shandon		1772-1904	1772-1956	1779-1960	RCB
St Finbarre's		1753-1897	1752-1928	1755-1787	RCB
St Luke's			1837-1875	1837-1845	LC, NA
		(chapel of ease, St Anne's Shandon)			
St Mary's Shandon		1671-1989	1669-1985	1684-1861	RCB
St Michael's		1828-1875	1828-1845	1828-1875	LC, NA
		(chapel of ease, St Finbarr's)			
St Nicholas		1723-1875	1723-1897	1726-1949	RCB
St Paul's		1798	1762-1820		ML
St Peter's		1745-1802	1751-1809		ML
Corkbeg	Cloyne	1836-1875	1838-1890	1836-1875	(LC), NA
Creagh	Ross				none
Cullen	Cork				none
Derryvillane	Cloyne				
Desertserges	Cork	1837-1875	1837-1845	1837-1875	(LC), NA
Desertmore	Cork				none
Dingindonavan	Cloyne	*see* Killeagh			
Donaghmore	Ross	*see* Abbeymanon			
Doneraile	Cloyne	1700-1900 (1,182)	1741-1895 (258)	1700-1899 (669)	MHC, *O'Kief*
Donoughmore	Cloyne		1845-1887 (25)	1899 (1)	MHC, *O'Kief*
Douglas	Cork	1789-1870	1792-1845	1803-1874	ML
Drimoleague	Cork	1812-1875	1812-1844	1812-1875	(LC), NA
Drinagh	Cork				none
Dromtarriff,Ardfert & Aghadoe					
Dunbolloge	Cork				
Dunderrow	Cork				
Dungourney	Cloyne		1850-1954		RCB
Durrus & Kilcrohane Cork					
Fanlobbus	Cork	1855-1871		1855-1872	ML
Farrihy	Cloyne		1845-1898 (16)		MHC
Fermoy	Cloyne	1800-1899(1,869)	1838-1899 (1,186)	1800-1899 (679)	MHC, *O'Kief*
Frankfield	Cork		1847-1955		RCB

Church of Ireland

Parish	Diocese	Baptisms	Marriages	Deaths	Location
Garrane-Kinnefeake	Cloyne	1850-1882	1859-1881	1875-1876	ML
Garrycloyne	Cloyne				none
Glanworth	Cloyne	1846-1881 (10)			MHC
Glengariffe	Cork	1863-1913			ML
Gortroe & Dysart	Cloyne		1846-1872 (8)		MHC
Ightermurragh	Cloyne				none
Inch	Cloyne				
Inchigeela	Cork	1900	1845-1884		RCB
Inchinabacky	Cloyne				none
Inniscarra	Cloyne	1820-1903	1820-1903	1852-1901	*O'Kief*
Innishannon	Cork	1693-1844	1693-1911	1693-1844	RCB
Inniskenny	Cork				none
Kanturk	Cloyne	1878-1899 (40)			MHC, *O'Kief*
Kilbonane	Cork				none
Kilbrin	Cloyne		1845-1898 (12)		MHC
Kilbrittain	Cork	1832-1876	1830-1868		RCB
Kilbrogan	Cork	1752-1872	1753-1853	1754-1877	RCB
Kilcoe	Ross				none
Kilcorney	Cloyne				
Kilcredan	Cloyne				none
Kilcully	Cork	1844-1880			(LC)
Kilfaughnabeg	Ross	1837-1877	1843-1844	1843-1856	
Kilgariffe	Ross				none
Kilkaskin	Ross				none
Kilkerranemore	Ross				
Killanully	Cork				
Killaspugmullane	Cork				none
Killeagh	Cloyne	1782-1880 (241)	1776-1879 (92)	1787-1868	RCB, (MHC)
Killeenemer	Cloyne				
Killowen	Cork	1832-1902		1851-1904	ML
Kilmacabea	Ross				none
Kilmaclenine	Cloyne				
Kilmahon	Cloyne				none
Kilmaloda	Ross				none
Kilmeen	Ross	1806-1876	1806-1845	1844-1876	LC
Kilmichael	Cork				none
Kilmocomoge	Cork				none
Kilmoe	Cork				none
Kilmurry	Cork	1878-1927	1848-1885	1879-1926	ML
Kilnagross	Ross				none
Kilnamartery	Cloyn				none
Kilroan	Cork	1885-1920	1846-1920		RCB
Kilshannick	Cloyne	1731-1899(1,908)	1845-1898 (86)	1731-1899 (1,107)	MHC, *O'Kief*
Kilteskin	Cloyne				

Church of Ireland

Parish	Diocese	Baptisms	Marriages	Deaths	Location
Kilworth	Cloyne	1887-1899 (23)	1845-1897 (35)	1887-1899 (33)	MHC
Kingston College	Cloyne				
Kinneigh	Cork				none
Kinsale	Cork	1684-1875	1688-1864	1685-1875	(LC), NA
Knockavilly	Cork	1837-1883	1844-1848		RCB
Knockmourne	Cloyne		1845-1890 (17)		MHC
Knocktemple	Cloyne	*see* Kilbolane			
Lackeen	Cloyne				
Leighmoney	Cork		1869-1943		RCB
Liscleary	Cork				
Lisgoold	Cloyne	1847-1871		1849-1875	ML
Lislee	Ross	1809-1900	1809-1902	1823-1917	ML
Litter	Cloyne	1811-1876	1811-1844	1811-1877	ML
Macroom	Cloyne	1727-1913	1727-1913	1837-1962	O'Kief
Magourney	Cloyne	1756-1876	1756-1844	1758-1876	ML
Mallow	Cloyne	1783-1956	1783-1956	1863-1915	*O'Kief*
Marmullane	Cork	1801-1873	1802-1954	1803-1873	RCB
Marshalstown	Cloyne	1831-1886	1832-1845	1849-1869	ML
Midleton	Cloyne	1699-1881	1728-1823	1696-1877	RCB
Mogeely	Cloyne				none
Mogeesha	Cloyne	1867-1875			ML
Monanimy	Cloyne	1812-1874	1814-1879	1824-1879	ML
Monkstown	Cork	1842-1875	1841-1845	1842-1875	LC, NA
Mourne Abbey	Cloyne	1832-1884 (53)	1847-1898 (15)	1850-1874 (5)	MHC, *O'Kief*
Moviddy	Cork	1877-1913	1848-1927	1878-1914	ML
Murragh	Cork				none
Myross	Ross				none
Nathlash	Cloyne	1844-1868 (12)			MHC
Nohaval	Cork	1785-1879	1785-1845	1784-1879	LC, NA
Queenstown *see* Clonmel					
Rahan	Cloyne		1847-1894 (13)	1881-1886 (12)	MHC
Rathbarry	Ross				
Rathclarin	Cork	1780-1875	1780-1849	1792-1875	RCB
Rathcooney	Cork	1750-1897	1749-1954	1750-1853	RCB
Rathcormac	Cloyne	1800-1899 (215)	1806-1897 (55)	1800-1899 (137)	MHC
Rincurran	Cork	1793-1875	1793-1845	1827-1875	LC, NA
Ringrone	Cork				none
Ross Cathedral	Ross	1690-1879	1690-1845	1690-1878	LC
Rostellan	Cloyne	1838-1861			ML
Shandrum	Cloyne				none
Skull	Cork				none
Subulter	Cloyne				'no church'
Taxax	Cork	1678-1679		1678-1679	ML
Templebodan	Cloyne	'entries of baptisms in Clonmult register'			
Templebredy	Cork				none

Church of Ireland

Parish	Diocese	Baptisms	Marriages	Deaths	Location
Templebryan	Ross			'no church, no records'	
Templemartin	Cork	1845-1893	1845-1902	1845-1912	ML
Templemichael	Cork		1845-1853		RCB
Templenacarriga	Cloyne	1885		1883-1932	RCB
Templeomalus	Ross	none			
Templequinlan	Ross	see Abbeymahon			
Templeroan	Cloyne				
Templetrine	Cork				none
Timoleague	Ross	1823-1900	1823-1900	1823-1910	Cork Co Libr
Tracton	Cork				none
Tullagh	Ross				none
Tullilease	Cloyne		1860 (1)		MHC
Wallstown	Cloyne	1824-1879			
Whitechurch	Cloyne		1848-1877 (8)		MHC
Youghal	Cloyne	1665-1874	1665-1845	1665-1874	LC, NA

Note: The register of Holy Trinity parish has been published: R. Caulfield, *The Register of the Parish of the Holy Trinity (Christ Church), Cork: from July 1643 to February 1668, with extracts from the Parish Books, from 1664 to 1668*, Cork, 1877

Marriage Licence Bonds

Some degree of compensation for the loss of the Church of Ireland parish registers is provided by the survival of indexes to the marriage licence bonds for the dioceses of Cork & Ross and Cloyne. The origin of these records merits brief mention. A dispensation to the practice in the Established Church of reading of banns before an intended marriage could be obtained by the granting of a marriage licence by the Church of Ireland bishop, which in turn required the parties to enter into an undertaking called a marriage licence bond. The surviving marriage licences and marriage licence bonds were destroyed in the 1922 Public Record Office fire, but fortunately, indexes survive for both Cork & Ross and Cloyne.

While these indexes represent only a portion of the Church of Ireland marriages and do not give a specific date or location, they do provide presumptive evidence of marriage and, in the absence of any other record, often the only evidence. The indexes name both the intending groom and bride and the year of the bond (which can be presumed to be the year of the marriage), e.g. 'Lawton, Hugh and Jane Kingston 1734'.

A block of entries for a specific surname in the indexes will often provide vital clues that enable the researcher to create a pedigree framework, especially if the surname is one of the less common ones. Though they include occasional Catholic marriages and Catholic parties to mixed marriages (not identified), the indexes should be assumed to be to non-Catholic marriages. There are four separate indexes, the originals of which are in the National Archives, but all are also available in printed form. The indexes in combination provide a record of over 30,000 marriages.

Index to the Marriage Licence Bonds of the Diocese of Cork & Ross for the years 1623 to 1750, edited by H. W. Gillman, Cork 1899-1900, also published in *O'Kief*, Vol. 4.
[Index to} Marriages, Diocese of Cork & Ross, 1716-1844 in *O'Kief*, vol. 4.
Index to the Marriage Licence Bonds of the Diocese of Cloyne for the years 1630 to 1800; edited by T. G. H. Green, Cork 1899-1900; also published in *O'Kief*, vol. 5.
[Index to] *Marriage Licence Bonds, Diocese of Cloyne, 1801-1866* in *O'Kief*, vol. 5.

GENERAL DIRECTORY.   67

O'Driscoll, Mrs. vintner, 20, Morgan street
   James, Rev. O. S. A. 2, Brunswick street
   Daniel, grocer, 5, Bridge street
O'Farrell & Newman, hardware men, 26, South main street,
O'Flynn, J. D. esq. M. D. 13, Hardwick street
Ogilvie, Peter, silk mercer and linen draper, 110, Patrick street
O'Grady, Jeremiah, merchant tailor,   33,   do.
   Mary Ann, dress maker, 39, Old George's street
O'Hallaran, William, accountant, 17, White street
O'Hara, Henry, silk mercer and haberdasher, 34, Patrick street
   William & Co printers and stationers, 53,   do.
O'Hea, James & Son, corn factors, 25, Cook street and Adelaide place
   Rev. Charles O. S. A. 2, Brunswick street
O'Keeffe, Thomas, Very Rev. V. G. R. C. archdeacon, 53, Douglas street
   Stephen, letter press printer, 44, South main street
   Thomas, sen. car owner, 8,   do.
   Alexander, white smith, 4, Curtis street
   William, hatter, 84, South main street
   Daniel, vintner, 2, Church street
   Michael, vintner, 30, Draw bridge street
   William, esq. attorney, 21, Cook street
   John,   do. 32, Clarence street
   Daniel,   do. 91, Great Britain street
   Michael, do.   1, John street

Extract from Jackson's "County & City of Cork Post Office General Directory", Cork 1843.

Chapter 11   Commercial & Postal Directories

As a historical record, directories, encompassing postal, commercial and trade directories and almanacs, are an illuminating and valuable source for both local historian and genealogist, but for the latter, they can have some limitations, especially in relation to the searcher's expectations. Even the most comprehensive nineteenth century Cork directories list only a small proportion of all heads of household and the criteria that might exclude an ancestor are often difficult to identify. As is also the case with newspapers and a range of other sources, the genealogical value of directories increases significantly for social groups above the lower middle class and they are of negligible value at the lower strata that includes manual, non-skilled and agricultural labourers, smallholders, fishermen and industrial workers. It is also worth noting that occupational listings such as 'cooper', 'tailor', etc. can almost always be interpreted as referring to master craftsmen (especially in cities and large towns), whose employees will be sought in vain in the same pages.

The earliest Cork directories are for Cork City — and in a few cases, selected county towns. Lucas's 1787 directory covers six towns in addition to Cork City, and Pigot's 1820 and 1824 directories provide similar coverage. Prior to 1875, however, no Cork directory covers the small towns and villages of rural County Cork in any depth and even in these later directories, the category 'principal landholders', i.e. farmers, has nebulous boundaries of inclusion and exclusion.

Lest one 'damn with faint praise' directories as a genealogical source, it is only fair to say that they are an excellent source of information on the middle class and upwards, and from the 1860s onwards a valuable guide to officialdom. They are a window into social and commercial life in nineteenth century communities and may often provide confirmation of oral tradition regarding employers and landlords. For those making a broad search for a rare or unusual surname, directories can provide a useful starting point and, if fruitful, valuable social background. Conversely, the search for McCarthy or Murphy ancestors is no less confusing when conducted in directories than in other sources.

Perusal of the full range of extant Cork directories is a task as daunting as the search for an elusive ancestor. Original copies of pre-1900 local directories survive in very small numbers and no single repository has a complete collection. While Cork libraries and the National Library are the most obvious locations, some less likely locations are cited in the *Waterloo Directory,* 1986. *Irish Genealogy, A Record Finder,* 1981, and J. Grenham's *Tracing Your Irish Ancestors,* 1992, provide more expansive notes on directories as a genealogical source.

The following list is comprehensive but not exhaustive, excluding directories or almanacs that are deemed not of genealogical value. Locations are cited only if the item appears to be rare. Bibliographic evidence of the publication of a directory in years other than those cited has been ignored if no publicly-held copy has been identified.

1758, 1769-70: 'A Brief Directory of the City of Cork, 1758 [and] 1769-70' by Wallace Clare, in *The Irish Genealogist*, vol. 1, no. 8, 1940, pp. 254-259. This is a compilation based on contemporary newspaper adverts and news items. The 1758 item, as published, covers the letters A-K only.

1787: *The Cork Directory for the Year 1787*
This directory by Richard Lucas covers Cork City and the towns of Bandon, Cove, Innishannon, Kinsale, Passage and Youghal. The city directory lists over 1,000 names and the towns directory totals approximately 350 names. The city directory was reprinted in the *Journal of the Cork Historical and Archaeological Society*, vol. 72, 1967, pp. 135-157; the directory of the six towns was reprinted in *The Irish Genealogist*, vol. 4, no. 1, 1968, pp. 37-46. Both are republished also in *O'Kief*.

1795: *The new Cork Directory for the year 1795...to which is added a correct list of the Freemen at Large*
This directory, printed by James Haly, is similar in coverage to Lucas, but the unalphabetised list of freemen is a useful appendix. Freemen at large were not necessarily residents of the city.

1803 (approx.)**:** *The New Cork Guide: containing the names and dwellings of the distinguished inhabitants...*
This publication, by Wm R. O'Connor, is included for curiosity value only; it consists of ten pages in verse. It is available in the National Library.

1809: *Holden's Triennial Directory*
(National Library)

1810: *Directory and Picture of Cork and its Environs*
by William West

1812: *Cork Directory for the Year 1812... containing an alphabetical list of the bankers, merchants and traders...*
This volume, by John Connor, covers Cork City only; about 2,100 names are included.

1817: *Cork Directory for the Year 1817...*
By John Connor as above but expanded to 2,500 names.

1820: *Commercial Directory of Ireland...* (Pigot's)
The volume by J. Pigot, includes directories of nobility, gentry and traders for Cork, Bandon, Kinsale and Youghal.

1824: *City of Dublin and Hibernian Provincial Directory* (Pigot's)
New expanded edition of J. Pigot' directory, it covers Cork City and 24 County Cork towns.

1826: *Cork Directory for the Year 1826*
By John Connor, it covers Cork City only; it provides almost 3,000 names; lists of streets and lanes in each city parish are included.

1842-43: *County and City of Cork Post Office General Directory*
By F. Jackson; the city coverage includes 3,500 names and is wide-ranging, but the county coverage of 1,750 names in a single alphabetical sequence is confined to nobility, gentry and clergy. A reprint was published in 1996 by the Library of Australian History, Sydney. A further edition under the same title was published by Alex. Aldwell for 1844-45.

1846: *Slater's National Commercial Directory of Ireland*
Slater was the successor to the Pigot series. The geographical range of Cork entries is in line with Pigot's 1824 edition. Further editions of Slater were published in 1856, 1870, 1881 and 1894. The range of coverage varied only slightly from edition to edition until the 1894 edition which had entries at parish level as well as towns.

1851: *Queenstown Directory and General Advertiser*
Nos 1-4, June-September 1851: 'A register of all that concerns Queenstown', it was published in broadsheet. It is available at the British Newspaper Library, Colindale.

1852: *Purcell's Commercial Cork Almanac*
This publication ran intermittently under slightly varied titles until 1934. The Boole Library, UCC has extensive holdings.

1863: *Robert H. Laing's Cork Mercantile Directory*
This covers Cork City only. It provides a street directory, an alphabetical listing of names and a trade directory.

1867: *Henry and Coghlan's General Directory of Cork, with Wynne's Business Directory of the Principal Towns*
Cork city and 18 towns are covered; however, no town west of Bandon is included.

1871: *Fulton's City of Cork Directory, Incorporating the Commercial Directory of Queenstown*

1872: *Wilkie's Cork City Directory*

1875-76: *Guy's County and City of Cork Directory*
This is a superb directory. While earlier directories confined themselves to the city and the large towns, this one lists gentry, clergy, schools, professions and trades people for the whole county, arranged by postal district. If the postal district is not immediately evident, access can be made through the alphabetical indexes of persons for the city and the county, about 5,00 and 10,000 names respectively.

1886: *Guy's Postal Directory of Munster*
Though similar in range to their '75-76 directory, this one lacks indexes and administrative material.

1889: *Guy's City and County Cork Almanac and Directory*
This directory was issued annually thereafter until 1935. It always included an alphabetical directory for the city; only on rare occasions for the county. The 1897 edition listed over 7,000 names for Cork city and almost 19,000 for the county.

1938: *Cork City and County Official Directory and Almanac*
This was published until 1946 by Paramount.

Chapter 12   Newspapers

Like the sirens of legend, newspapers beckon the family historian into a promised land of marriage notices, obituaries and other genealogically-rewarding news items, but the rewards for the optimistic researcher may not be equal to the time consumed in the search. However, newspapers, if often the least rewarding of the genealogical sources, are also the most interesting, for even when the object of the search is not located, the reader is entertained and informed.

The focus of many researchers' forays into newspaper sources will be the births, marriages and deaths columns, but these notices have historically been so socially stratified that their value to anyone of humble descent will be negligible. Only a minute proportion of all marriages and deaths prior to the 1920s was published in newspapers and such notices as were published were predominantly of the gentry, merchant and middle class families. In the nineteenth century, the names of ordinary men and women were only recorded in newspaper columns in such unfortunate circumstances as death by misadventure or violence, as parties in litigation, as offenders against law, or as victims of eviction. In the absence of indexes to Cork newspapers comprehensive enough to record such minutiae of press reportage, newspaper searches are more often voyages of exploration than discovery.

Several collections of abstracts of birth, marriage and death notices published in Cork and Munster newspapers have been compiled (see below) and are an excellent genealogical source within the limitations outlined. Because it was common practice among provincial newspapers to copy such notices from each other's papers, an abstract of notices from a Kerry, Limerick or Waterford newspaper can be a valuable Cork genealogical source. The abstract of a notice may usually provide the detail one requires, but, where possible, it is wise to seek out the original item as published; the nature of newspaper abstracts and the abbreviations regularly used in compiling them can often result in relevant genealogical information being omitted.

Newspapers are, of course, the best source for getting an overview of the times in which an ancestor lived and are a fascinating window on the contemporary world they recorded. In that respect, they merit the attention of the family historian regardless of social background.

The personal columns apart, what potentially relevant information can the family researcher expect to find in Cork newspapers? Assizes and other criminal proceedings were reported, though often without accurate addresses in the pre-Famine period. Shipping movements were regularly updated and before the establishment of regular trans-Atlantic steamer routes, a regular seasonal feature of the shipping columns were advertisements for the imminent departure of sailing vessels for North American ports; lists of embarking emigrants were never published. Incidents of eviction and of land agitation were sometimes, but not always, reported in great detail. Testimonials to retiring officials and clergy, and lists of contributors to church building funds or other charitable causes were a feature of advertising columns in the later nineteenth century.

Selected List of County Cork Printed Newspapers, with Guide to Locations
(dates are for publication history, not necessarily extant files)

Newspaper Title	Years of Publication	British Newspaper Library	National Library of Ireland	Cork City Library	Cork County Library
Cork Journal	1753-72		1756-63 (m)	1756-63 (m)	
Cork Evening Post	1755-91		1767/69/81-91 (m)		
(then New Cork Evening Post)	1791-1806		1791-1806 (m)	1797	
Hibernian Chronicle	1768-1802		1769-1802	1769-1802 (m)	
(then Cork Mercantile Chronicle)	1802-1835	1832-35	1802-18/23/25-28	1802-18 (m)	1832-35 (m)
Cork Herald	1798-99				
(then Cork Advertiser)	1799-1823		1799-1823 (gaps)	1807	
Southern Reporter	1807-1871	1823-71	1807-08/17-18/ 26-27/29-32/34/56-71		1821-23, 24, 26-27 / 1830-33, 47
Cork Morning Intelligencer	1815-1823		1815-16		
Constitution	1822-1924	1826-1924	1822-24/27/29/31-34/ 1873-1922	1825-26/28-1922	
Cork Evening Herald	1833-1836	1833-36	1833-36 (m)		1833-36 (m)
(then Cork Standard & Ev. Hld)	1836-1841	1836-41			1837 (m)
Cork Weekly Times	1833-1834	1833-34	1833-34 (m)		1833-34 (m)
People's Press	1834-1836	1834-1836	1834-1836 (m)		1834-1836 (m)
Munster Advertiser	1839-1841	1839-41	1839-41 (m)		1839-41 (m)
Cork Examiner/The Examiner	1841-present	1841-present	1841-present	1841-1923/57-pres	1841-present (m)
Cork Herald	1856-1901	1858-1901	1870-74/96-01		
Skibbereen Eagle (later Cork County Eagle)	1857-1922	1861-1922	1881-84, 1899-1922		1861-1922 (m)
Southern Star (Skibbereen)	1890- present	1892-1919, 1935-73	1921-present	1969-present	1921-35 (m)
Evening Echo	1892-present	1896-1925, 1927-present	1927-present	1930-present	
Cork Weekly Examiner	1895-1981	1896-1981	1921-81		
Cork Sun	1903-1905	1903-1905	1903-05 (m)		1903-05 (m)
Cork Sportsman	1908-1911	1908-11	1908-11 (m)		1908-11 (m)
Cork Free Press	1910-1916	1910-16	1910-16		

As time progressed, newspapers, like society, became more 'democratic', but it was not until the second or third decade of the twentieth century that the insertion of death notices as paid advertisements in daily newspapers became a widespread practice. Obituaries, as distinct from death notices, are curiously irregular in appearance in Cork newspapers, even when the subject was of prominence in local society. Prior to the 1860s or 1870s, obituaries, if they did appear, were eulogistic and rarely contained information of genealogical value.

A feature of the Cork press that militates against its countywide value is that, with the singular exception of Skibbereen, no newspapers were published outside of Cork City until relatively recent times. Cork City newspapers were either poorly served by correspondents or not interested enough to report everyday occurrences in peripheral regions of the county such as the Beara peninsula, or the Duhallow region. The Skibbereen newspapers, whose extant files date back to 1861, had, conversely, a very local focus of attention until the early 1900s.

One of the ironies of newspaper searches in Cork, and in Ireland generally, is that the most comprehensive collection of nineteenth century newspapers will be found not in Cork or in Dublin, but in the British Newspaper Library at Colindale, London.

However, microfilm copies of newspapers are more widely available and the requirements of most researchers will probably be satisfied by the holdings of Cork libraries, which can between them offer at least one Cork newspaper for almost every year since 1769. Library newspaper holdings are increasingly only available for consultation on microfilm. A consequence of this for users is that access at any one time is limited to the number of microfilm reader units available in a library. This particularly applies to the Cork libraries. It is therefore advisable to check the availability of microfilm readers prior to a visit to Cork City or County Library for the purpose of newspaper research.

It is difficult to provide a satisfactory locations list for extant files of Cork newspapers within the scope of this publication. It is, indeed, usually the case that a complete file of many of the pre-1850 Cork papers does not exist and that the most complete file is in the aggregate holdings of two or more libraries. The most accurate comprehensive listing of Irish newspapers with principal locations is the Newsplan Report compiled for the National Library of Ireland and the British Library in 1992. Also worthy of consultation is the Waterloo Directory of Irish Newspapers, which provides general comments on the content and publishing history of a newspaper as well as locations. However, neither of these reference sources indicates all locations of microfilm copies of newspapers. The appended list of the principal Cork newspapers provides some indication of holdings outside of the National Library of Ireland and Colindale.

Over 50 newspapers, excluding title changes, have been published in Cork in the period 1750-1950. Many of them are irrelevant to genealogical research because of short publication history or lack of genealogical content. The principal late-eighteenth century newspapers were the Cork Evening Post and the Hibernian Chronicle (later Cork Mercantile Chronicle). The leading newspapers of the nineteenth century were the Southern Reporter, the Constitution (the leading Protestant conservative paper), the Cork Examiner and the Cork Herald. The latter was the first Cork newspaper to publish daily (1860). Prior to that, the leading newspapers were published three days a week.

Newspaper Abstracts

The title of a collection of abstracts can be misleading if interpreted literally. A collection of abstracts may be notices selected by the compiler to the exclusion of others and newspaper abstracts for a stated period may be only from surviving copies in that period, though such omissions will be stated or apparent in the body of the work. It should however be noted that these compilers had, on occasion, access to files not in the public domain. In the following list, abstracts from *O'Kief* are grouped together under descriptive titles not necessarily those used by the editor.

John T. Collins, Abstracts from Cork-printed newspapers 1753-1799 in *O'Kief*, Vol. 6, p. 2372ff.; Vol. 7, p. 1251ff (principally from *Cork Journal* 1761-77, *Cork Evening Post* 1789-99, *Hibernian Chronicle* 1769-1802).

Basil O'Connell, Abstracts from Cork-printed newspapers, 1801-1922 in *O'Kief*, Vol.7, p. 1546ff; Vol. 14, p. 2281ff (principally from *Cork Mercantile Chronicle*, 1802-28, *Cork Morning Intelligencer* 1816-21; *Southern Reporter*, 1817-34, 1868-71, *Constitution*, 1822-1922.)

Basil O'Connell, Births, marriages and deaths reported in the Kerry Evening Post, 1828-1917 in *O'Kief*, Vol. 6, p. 2064ff.; Vol. 11, p. 1ff, p. 2020ff; Vol. 15, p. 1161 ff.

Basil O'Connell, Births, marriages, deaths and miscellaneous events in Cork and Kerry abstracted from Limerick and other newspapers 1781-1872 in *O'Kief*, Vol. 8, p. 2385ff.; Vol. 11, p. 46ff (principally from *Limerick Chronicle*, 1781-1840, *Limerick Evening Post*, 1811-17, 1828-31).

Basil O'Connell, Abstracts from the *Cork Examiner*, 1923-1948 in *O'Kief*, Vol. 15 p. 2331 ff.

H. F. Morris, Abstracts of births, deaths and marriages in Waterford newspapers 1771-1796 in *IG*, Vols 4-6, 1973-1982 (taken from *Ramsey's Waterford Chronicle*, 1771, '76-'78, '86-88, '91; *Waterford Herald*, 1791-94, 1796) — with indexes.

H. F. Morris, Extracts from *Finn's Leinster Journal* 1767-1770 in *IG*, Vol. 6, No. 5, 1984 - Vol. 8, No. 4, 1993 (newspaper published in Kilkenny).

Rosemary ffolliott, Index to biographical notices collected from newspapers, principally relating to Cork and Kerry, 1756-1827 (the most systematic and user-friendly of newspaper abstracts, because it is arranged in card index form with a full transcription of each notice.) The National Library and the Boole Library (UCC) have copies of the original card index. Cork City Library has a microfilm copy.

Rosemary ffolliott, Index to biographical notices in the newspapers of Limerick, Ennis, Clonmel and Waterford, 1758-1821.

IGRS: Card indexes to biographical notices in the *Hibernian Chronicle* (1771-1802) and the *Cork Mercantile Chronicle* (1802-1818) are held by the IGRS library in London.

References and further reading

Newsplan: Report of the Newsplan Project in Ireland, compiled by J. O'Toole, London, Dublin, British Library/National Library of Ireland, 1992
The Waterloo Directory of Irish Newspapers and Periodicals, 1800-1900: Phase II, by J. S. North, Waterloo, Ontario, North Waterloo Academic Press,1986
R. ffolliott 'Newspapers as a Genealogical Source', in *Irish Genealogy: A Record Finder*, ed. D. Begley, Dublin, 1981
R. ffolliott, 'Matched and Dispatched', in IG vol.3, No. 7, 1962, pp.
H. F. Morris, 'Beginner's Page: Newspapers', in *IG* Vol. 6, No. 4, 1983
Tim Cadogan, 'Cork Newspapers — their history', in *The Southern Star Centenary 1889-1989*, Skibbereen, 1989

Chapter 13 Records of the Graveyard

Civil registration of deaths in Ireland dates from 1864. If the approximate dates of death of ancestors have been deduced, these can be verified through searches of the death indexes, but the process can be time-consuming and requires the elimination of persons of similar name and locality. That it may circumvent this search process is among the attractions of locating an ancestral gravestone inscription. Of course, if that elusive gravestone predates 1864, it may take the researcher back beyond the earliest documentary sources. It must be remarked here that this is a journey to be undertaken more in hope than in confidence.

Cork county has in excess of 600 graveyards. For many of these burial grounds, the only record of those interred there are the gravestone inscriptions, which in turn record the names of only a small proportion of the total population of the graveyard. The families of prosperous tenant farmers, merchants, professionals, etc. will be represented, but the 'men of no property' and their families invariably lie in unmarked graves. Many of the older disused rural graveyards have been untended for over a generation and are, especially in summertime when vegetation is lushest, a daunting obstacle to those seeking an elusive gravestone.

A prerequisite of the search for a gravestone inscription is identification of the burial place of a family. This may not be difficult if one is researching a family group that had a long and permanent association with a locality, but such is not always the case. The burial place of a family may represent their place of residence/origin a generation or two earlier than the period with which one is familiar and may be in the adjoining parish or further afield. For this reason it is always advisable when interviewing elderly relatives to ascertain any surviving tradition concerning place of burial; the significance of such information can be of paramount importance at a later stage.

Civil records will give no indication of place of burial, but for persons who died after 1900, it may be worthwhile, in instances where a date of death is known, to search local newspapers for a death notice. This will usually name the place of burial. For further comments on published death notices, see the section on newspaper sources (Chapter 12).

If one has identified a cemetery that merits investigation, there are potentially three 'records' that can be sought, viz., a burial register, the gravestones, and finally a transcript or recording of the gravestone inscriptions in the cemetery.

Burial registers for County Cork graveyards can generally be said not to predate 1890 and if the burial ground is disused, may not be extant, or in the case of the older graveyards, may never have existed. Exceptions to this are newer burial grounds established in the twentieth century and, generally, the large municipal cemeteries. St Finbarr's Cemetery, Cork City's principal cemetery, opened in 1869, has comprehensive and well-maintained registers of burials for its entire history, but is the exception in this regard. Rural graveyards do not have permanent caretakers and it is best to enquire locally to ascertain if a register is likely to exist.

The quality and legibility of gravestone inscriptions will vary from region to region. The unsuitability of local stone for gravestones can result in some areas having a low density of memorials. Where the stone used was unsuitable to combat weathering, one of the effects is that old gravestone inscriptions have become unreadable. Gravestones are environmentally fragile despite their contrary appearance and in attempting to decipher inscriptions, it should be stressed that no chemical cleaning agent or wire brush should be used to clean the stone's surface. Carry a supply of chalk with you on a visit and rub the chalk along the line of the inscription. This will highlight the lettering sufficiently to enable a reading to be made.

Gravestone inscriptions had attracted the attention of antiquarians long before there was any systematic attempt made by genealogists to record them. Between 1888 and 1937, the Association for the Preservation of the Memorials of the Dead (a title redolent of Victorian antiquarianism) published in their journal thousands of inscriptions recorded in graveyards throughout Ireland. The value to the family historian of those records is limited by several factors. Contributors had a tendency to 'cherry pick' the oldest, the most impressive or the most historically significant gravestones in a cemetery, often to the exclusion of , or even comment on, the cemetery's other gravestones. Geographical coverage was also haphazard, being greatly influenced by the place of residence of contributors; and in too many cases, inscriptions have been shown to have been either transcribed or printed inaccurately.

In County Cork, the most systematic and authoritative recording of inscriptions is that made by Richard Henchion, whose transcripts, with annotation, of the inscriptions in 16 Cork graveyards were published in the *Journal of the Cork Historical and Archaeological Society,* from 1967 to 1990. These provide the standard to which all recordings of inscriptions should aspire, but which, unfortunately, relatively few achieve. The inscriptions in over 20 graveyards in mid and north Cork were published in *O'Kief;* these, while more comprehensive than the Memorials of the Dead, are somewhat lacking in reliability. The recording of gravestone inscriptions has been included among community employment schemes, sponsored by FÁS (Training and Employment Authority) and by other government agencies, undertaken since the mid-1980s. The quality of these projects has been widely variant and only a minority of them have been formally published; however it is worth enquiring locally if a survey of this type has been undertaken for local cemeteries. A small number of gravestone inscription records have been published in monograph-form or as journal articles, based in some cases on surveys undertaken by community schemes, and in some cases as a result of independent surveys.

In the following list, brief citations are provided, identifying source and date of publication. Authors/compilers are identified only where necessary for retrieval; all *Journal of the Cork Historical and Archaeological Society (JCHAS)* references are to articles by Richard Henchion. Items described as 'typescript' or 'Mss' are unpublished, but a copy is located at Cork County Library and/or Cork City Library. The name of the cemetery recorded is followed, in brackets, by the name of the civil parish in which it is located, unless both names are the same.

The Irish Genealogical Research Society (IGRS) initiated a programme in 1972 to record gravestone inscriptions prior to 1880 throughout Ireland, and invited participants to submit copies of recordings to the IGRS Tombstone Committee, c/o The Genealogical Office, Kildare Street, Dublin. The principal respondent from County Cork was a youth group in the Beara area working under the supervision of local historian D. M. O'Brien. Their 1975 compilation was transcribed with supplementary material in 1996 by Beara Historical Society and is listed below under 'Beara'. A listing of County Cork gravestone inscriptions in *Tracing Your Irish Ancestors* by John Grenham includes the separate entries for Beara graveyards and other contributions to the IGRS programme not listed below.

List of Gravestone Inscription Transcripts

Aghinagh: *JCHAS*, Vol. 72, 1967

Ballinacurra (Middleton): *JCHAS*, Vol 95, 1990

Ballincollig Military (Carrigrohane): Henchion & Rice (comp) 1995, typescript

Ballyclogh: *O'Kief*, vol. 8, 1965

Ballycurrany: *JCHAS*, Vol. 83, 1978

Ballydesmond (Nohavaldaly): A. T. Culloty, *Ballydesmond, A Rural Parish in its Historical Setting,* pp289-299, Dublin, 1986

Ballymodan: *Ballymodan, Bandon, County Cork Gravestone Inscriptions,* and, *St Peter's Ballymodan, County Cork Gravestone Inscriptions* (Genealogical Survey of Bandon S. 1985)

Ballynoe: *Ballynoe Cemetery: a guide and brief history* (1993)

Ballyvourney: *O'Kief*, Vol. 6, 1963

Banteer (Clonmeen): *O'Kief*, Vol. 7

Bantry (Kilmocomogue): IGRS Collection, Genealogical Office

Bantry Abbey (Kilmocomogue): IGRS Collection, Genealogical Office

Bantry, St Finbarr's (Kilmocomogue): IGRS Collection, Genealogical Office

Beara Peninsula: (Barony of Bere) in *Heritage of the Graveyard: the gravestone inscriptions in the Barony of Bere,* compiled 1975, 2nd edition 1996, Beara Historical Society

Bere Island (Killaconenagh): *St Michael's, Bere Island: Gravestone Inscriptions,* Bere Island Heritage, 1996

Buttevant: in Mallow Heritage Centre

Carrigrohanebeg: *JCHAS*, Vol. 78, 1968

Castlemagner: *O'Kief*, Vol. 6, 1963

Charleville: (Rathgoggan); *O'Kief*, Vol. 11, 1966

Clondrohid: *O'Kief*, Vol. 6, 1963

Clonfert: *O'Kief*, Vol. 6, 1963

Clonmeen: *O'Kief*, Vol. 7, 1964

Clonmel: L.Cassidy (ed.), *Clonmel (Old Church), Cobh, 1698-1984,* Cobh, 1984

Clonmult: *JCHAS*, Vols 81-82, 1976-77

Coachford (Magourney): *O'Kief*, Vol. 11, 1966

Cork Military (Cork City): D. Harvey & G. White, *The Barracks: a history of Victoria/Collins Barracks, Cork*, 1997, pp. 232-234

Cullen (Barony of Duhallow): *O'Kief*, Vol. 6, 1963

Cullen (Barony of Kinsale): Cullen (Ballymartle), *JCHAS*, Vol. 94, 1989

Dangandonovan: *JCHAS*, Vol. 79, 1974

Desertmore: *JCHAS*, Vol. 79, 1974

Doneraile: Power & Sleeman, 'The Church of Ireland, Doneraile', in *Mallow Field Club Journal*, No. 10, 1992, pp. 73-94; *O'Kief*, Vol. 11, 1966

Douglas (Cork City): 'Inscriptions/Burials, St Luke's Church of Ireland Graveyard, Douglas, County Cork', 1987, typescript

Drishane: *O'Kief*, Vol. 6, 1963

Dromagh (Dromtarriff): *O'Kief*, Vol. 6, 1965

Dromtarriff: *O'Kief*, Vol. 6, 1963,Vol. 8, 1965

Dunderrow: *JCHAS*, Vol. 76, 1971

Fermoy Military: N. Brunicardi, 'Military Burials in Old Fermoy Graveyard', in *Irish Sword*, No. 51, 1977, pp. 162-5; No. 53, 1979 p. 382

Glanworth: *St Dominick's Old Cemetery, Glanworth: history and inscriptions*, Glanworth Community Council/Fás, 1990-91

Inchigeela: *O'Kief*, Vol. 6, 1963

Kilbrin: O'Kief, Vol. 8, 1965

Kilbrogan: 'Kilbrogan Church of Ireland, Bandon Gravestone Inscriptions' and 'Kilbrogan R. C. Bandon Gravestone Inscriptions', Genealogical Survey of Bandon S., 1985

Kilcorcoran: *O'Kief*, Vol. 7, 1964

Kilcorney: *O'Kief*, Vol. 7, 1964

Kilcrea Abbey: (Desertmore); *JCHAS*, Vol. 73, 1968

Kilgrogan: *O'Kief*, Vol. 11, 1966

Killeagh: *JCHAS*, Vols 77, 78, 1972, '73

Killeens (Rahan): *see* Rahan

Killingley (Killanully): 'Killingley (or Killanully) gravestone inscriptions', undated typescript

Kilmeen: *O'Kief*, Vol. 6, 1963

Kilmonogue: *JCHAS*, Vol. 92, 1987

Kilmurry: O'Mahony & Sheehan, 'Gravestone Inscriptions in Kilmurry (South) Graveyard', undated manuscript, Cork County Library

Kilnaglory: *JCHAS*, Vol. 74, 1969

Kilnamartyra: *O'Kief*, Vol. 6, 1963

Kinsale: J. L. Darling, *St Multose Church, Kinsale*, Cork , 1895, memorial plaques, etc, pp. 27-43

Kiskeam: (Kilmeen); *O'Kief*, Vol. 6, 1963

Knocknagree: (Nohavaldaly); *O'Kief*, Vol. 6, 1963

Liscarroll: *O'Kief*, Vol. 11, 1966

Lisgoold: *JCHAS*, Vol. 83, 1978

Lyre (Clonmeen): *O'Kief*, Vol. 7, 1964

Macloneigh: *O'Kief*, Vol. 8, 1965

Macroom: *O'Kief*, Vol. 8, 1965, and Vol. 14

Mallow: J. Caplice, 'St James' Church, Mallow', in *Mallow Field Club Journal*, No. 8, 1990; 'St James' Cemetery, Mallow', in *Mallow Field Club Journal*, No. 8, 1990: 'St Mary's Cemetery, Mallow', in *Mallow Field Club Journal*, No. 13, 1995

Marmullane: C. O'Mahony 'Gravestone Inscriptions of Marmullane Churchyard, Passage West, County Cork', 1990, typescript

Midleton: *Canon B. Troy, The Cemetery: Church of Our Lady of the Most Holy Rosary, Midleton; gravestone inscription*, Midleton, 1994

Millstreet (Drishane): *O'Kief*, Vol. 6, 1963

Mitchelstown (Brigown): 'Mitchelstown Community Council/AnCo Heritage Survey — St George's Graveyard', 1988, typescript

Molagga (Aghacross): Rev. W. Clare in *IG*, vol. 2, No. 12, 1955, pp 390-393; and K. Hanley et al, *Archaeological Survey of St Molagga's Church, Aghacross*, pp. 35-47, Cork, 1994

Mourne Abbey: *O'Kief*, Vol. 11, 1966

Newmarket: (Clonfert); *O'Kief*, vol. 6, 1963

Nohavaldaly: *O'Kief*, Vol. 8, 1965

Quaker: (Cork City); 'Quaker Graveyard, Summerhill South, Cork: inscriptions', typescript, Cork, 1987

Rahan: 'Rahan and Killeens Cemeteries', in *Mallow Field Club Journal*, No. 7, 1989, pp. 99-114

Rockchapel (Clonfert): *O'Kief*, Vol. 8, 1965

St Peter's (Cork City): *JCHAS*, Vol. 93, 1988

Timoleague: Mss. 622, Genealogical Office

Tisaxon: *JCHAS*, Vol. 75, 1979

Titeskin: *JCHAS*, Vol. 75, 1970

Tullylease: *O'Kief*, Vol. 8, 1965

Youghal: S. Hayman, *The Handbook for Youghal, Youghal*, 1896, reprinted 1973; selected inscriptions from plaques and memorials

Chapter 14   Electoral Lists

The annually updated register of electors is nowadays the most comprehensive publicly-available record of adult population, but its currency means that it only rarely proves a useful tool in genealogical research. Universal adult suffrage in Ireland dates from 1923, a date still considered too recent to be of value to the vast majority of researchers. Prior to 1923, however, the electorate represents a decreasing proportion of total population. The Cork City electorate represented 43.9 percent of population in 1918, 13.9 percent in 1885 and only 3.9 percent on the eve of the 1832 Reform Act. Ironically, it is from that early period that most surviving nineteenth century Cork electoral material dates.

Most of this material consists not of official electoral lists but of published lists of voters and their electoral preferences or in the case of the Youghal records, of the more official, but similar poll books. These records predate the introduction of the secret ballot in 1872. Their genealogical value varies as the amount of detail provided differs from one to another. It might be expected that these records are exclusively dealing with the upper echelons of society, but in some cases at least, this is not so. The occupational breakdown of the 1835 Cork City list is:

Gentlemen:	16.4%
Professionals:	8.3%
Merchants, etc.:	9.1%
Shopkeepers:	12.8%
Publicans, etc:	7.1%
Artisans:	20.1%
Farmers:	15%
Labourers:	9.3%
Others:	1.9%

Electoral Lists

Cork 1818: *A full report of the proceedings at the election for the City of Cork 1818...*, Cork, 1818. Lists 1,388 voters and their preferences are interspersed through the report. First name initial only, no occupation.
(Cork County Library)

Cork 1826: *Lists of the freemen and freeholders, alphabetically arranged, who voted at the Cork election, December 1826,* Cork 1826. List, in two sequences, of 1,989 voters with addresses and, in many cases, occupations.
(Cork County Library)

Cork 1829: *A full report of the election for the City of Cork...July 1829,* Cork, 1829. Lists of 657 voters interspersed in text; no addresses or occupations given.
(Cork County Library)

Cork 1830: *Proceedings of the election for the City of Cork...August 1830,* Cork 1830. Names of 1,651 voters interspersed in text; addresses, but no occupations.
(Cork County Library)

Cork 1835: Lists of voters at the Cork City election 1835 in *People's Press and Cork Weekly Register,* January 17- February 14, 1835. Names, addresses and, in many cases, occupations of over 3,200 voters. Not in alphabetical sequence.

Bandon 1832: Bandon electors 1832 in *Seanchas Chairbre,* no. 2, 1983, pp. 31-37; also published in *Cork County Eagle,* 3 July, 1915. Names, addresses and occupations of 233 voters at the 1832 election.

Youghal 1835, 1837: 'Borough politics in O'Connellite Ireland: the Youghal Poll Books of 1835 and 1837', ed A. Barry and K. T. Hoppen in *Journal of the Cork Historical and Archaeological Society,* vol. 83, 1978, pp. 106-46 and vol. 84, 1979, pp. 15-43. Names, addresses, occupations of 267 voters in 1835 and 308 in 1837.

The survival rate of electoral registers for the post-Famine period is very poor; no register or list of electors of genealogical value appears to be extant between 1840 and 1900. The situation post -1900 is slightly better as registers of electors for Cork city for 1900-03 inclusive, 1911 and 1913 are extant and are held by the National Archives.

A related source is the list of Applications for the Registering of Freeholds which was published in the *Southern Reporter* newspaper in May-June 1829. Approximately 1,250 applicants are listed by name, address, and description of the freehold in respect of which they were applying. Occupation is sometimes included. Those applying included both farmers and towndwellers. A copy of the list, with a partial index, is available in Cork County Library.

Chapter 15   Occupational Sources

It is always advantageous to know the profession or occupation of an ancestor, though the value accruing from that knowledge varies according to the occupation. One will hope that it provides at least some avenue of research beyond the standard primary sources, but it should be noted that in the most common occupations, little further source material will be available, as the 'paper trail' left by subsistence farmers, agricultural and industrial labourers, shop assistants and casual labourers prior to 1900 is regrettably sparse. Conversely, those in professions such as the law and medicine and in upper middle class occupations are likely to be well documented in archival and secondary sources.

The sources cited are primarily printed sources of specific Cork interest or of national interest with significant Cork content and include both the 'list of names' approach and guides to archival sources for specific occupations. An exhaustive survey of archival sources being beyond the compass of this work, reference to such sources is selective, being limited to published literature or reference to occupations deemed particularly relevant.

Army

The necessary sources for tracing an ancestor in the British Army are in British archives. Archival guides include the Public Record Office Reader's Guides, *Army Records for Family Historians* by S. Fowler, London, 1992, and *Records of the Militia from 1757* by G. Thomas, London, 1993. It has been estimated that as many as 20,000 natives of Cork enlisted in the British Army in 1914-18. Approximately ten percent of them died in action and are recorded in *Ireland's Memorial Records*, 8 vols. See also *Soldiers died in the Great War* series, Part 72: 'Royal Munster Fusiliers', and 'Cork-born soldiers who died in World War I from *Ireland's Memorial Records*' in *Times Past*, Vol. 7, 1990-91.

Board of Ordnance: J. A. Acton (ed), 'Employees at Board of Ordnance establishments in Ireland in 1815', in *The Irish Genealogist*, Vol. 6, Nov. 1985, pp. 788-813.

This listing includes tradesmen, labourers, etc, at Cork Harbour construction works and employees at the gunpowder factory in Ballincollig, County Cork. Details given include year of birth, marital status, number of children and occupation. Almost 800 of the 1,263 employees listed had County Cork addresses.

Church of Ireland Clergy

W. M. Brady's *Clerical and Parochial Records of Cork, Cloyne and Ross*, 3 vols, Dublin, 1863-64, includes excellent genealogical notes on clerical families serving in County Cork Church of Ireland parishes from the seventeenth century.

Brady is updated to the year 1903 by J. H. Cole's *Church and Parish Records of the United Diocese of Cork Cloyne and Ross*, Cork, 1903.

Clock/Watchmakers

R. ffolliott, 'Biographical notes on some Cork Clock and watchmakers', in *Journal of the Cork Historical and Archaeological Society*, Vol. 69, 1964, pp. 38-55. The article contains over 160 entries of varying length, some of which (e.g. Montjoy) are rich in genealogical notes.

Doctors

Members of the Medical profession will be found well represented in sources such as directories, newspapers and wills. An appendix 'Biographical notes on Doctors of Physick and Chyrurgeons in Cork' to C. J. F. MacCarthy's article 'Patrick Blair, MD' in *JCHAS*, Vol. 90, 1985 is informative on Cork doctors of the eighteenth and early nineteenth centuries. N. M. Cummins' *Some Chapters of Cork Medical History*, Cork, 1957, lists those doctors who were on the staff in Cork City's hospitals in the nineteenth century.

Goldsmiths

M. S. D. Westropp, 'The Goldsmiths of Cork' in *Journal of the Cork Historical and Archaeological Society*,Vol. 8, 1902, pp. 37-43.

Legal Profession

E. Keane et al (eds), *King's Inns Admission Papers 1607-1867*, Dublin, 1986. This book provides valuable source information on attorneys and barristers, citing father's name, address, occupation, mother's maiden name, age, etc, though not all of these in every case. See page 86.

Merchant Seamen

Archival sources for maritime history are the focus of a special maritime issue of *Irish Archives: Journal of the Irish Society for Archives*, vol. 2, no. 1, Summer 1992. A valuable guide to sources of genealogical value is Nicholas Cox's 'The Records of the Registrar General of Shipping and Seamen' in *Maritime History*, vol. 2, no. 2, September 1972, pp. 168-188. F. P. Murphy, 'In Pursuit of Seafaring Ancestors' in *Decies* , no. 17, May 1981, pp. 53-56, is an interesting 'hands on' research report.

In the 1875, 1886 and 1890s Guy's Postal Directories, under the general heading 'Port of Cork', there are official lists of the river and harbour pilots and steamship captains licensed by the Harbour Commissioners. The 1875 and 1886 lists include pilots from the ports of Kinsale, Crookhaven, etc. and the lists for 1886 and 1897 give the ages of the pilots.

In a series of articles which he contributed to JCHAS (Vol. 1, 1895; Vol. 23, 1917; Vol. 25, 1919) on the history of Port of Cork steamships and steam navigation, W. J. Barry has many references to steamship captains associated with

Cork Harbour shipping and in the case of vessels lost during the First World War provides lists of crewmen lost and saved.

Navy

Substantial numbers of Corkmen joined the Royal Navy during the nineteenth and early twentieth century. Almost twenty percent of Irish-born officers in the Royal Navy during the Napoleonic Wars were from Cork and the proportion on the lower deck was probably much higher. Royal Navy official records, including those of the Coastguard Services, are located at the Public Record Office, London, and are comprehensively listed and explained in N. M. Rodger, *Naval Records for Genealogists*, PRO Handbooks, No. 22, London, HMSO, 1988. Lists of Irish officer entrants to the Navy during the Napoleonic Wars are published in *The Irish Genealogist*, vol. 3, nos 11 and 12 and *The Irish Ancestor*, vol. 1, no. 1, 1969.

Nurserymen

E. McCracken, 'Notes on eighteenth century Irish nurserymen', in *Irish Forestry*, Vol. 24, No. 1, pp. 39-53.

Police

Comprehensive coverage of the genealogical sources for researching the 80,000 members of Ireland's pre-1922 police force is provided by Jim Herlihy's *The Royal Irish Constabulary: A Short History and Genealogical Guide*, Dublin, 1997

Tradesmen

Sean Daly's appendix to his *Cork: a City in Crisis*, Cork, 1978, is a valuable résumé of the trades and trade societies of Cork from 1700 to 1870. As he observes, documentary remains of the societies are sparse, but records of Cork Typographical Society (from 1868), the Cork Coopers' Society (from 1870) and the Cork Plumbers Society (1868-94) are extant and are held by the Cork Archives Institute.

24   KING'S INNS

BARRY, JOHN SHERIDAN TOTTENHAM, 6th s. of Laurence, Douglas Street, Cork, and Margaret Powell; over 16; ed. Cork; afft. father. H 1836.

BARRY, JOSEPH, attorney, n.d. [? c 1674].

BARRY, JOSEPH, 1st s. of Joseph, Mallow, Co. Cork, Doctor of Physic, decd., and Eliza Leader. M.T., M 1788. E 1791.

BARRY, KINGSMILL, attorney King's Bench, T 1756.

BARRY, MATHEW, attorney Chancery, M 1759.

BARRY, MICHAEL, solicitor Chancery c 1734.

BARRY, MICHAEL, s. and heir of John, Rathrush, Co. Carlow. M.T., H 1724. T 1736, d. July 1745. [Prerog. Will Michael Barry, Rathrush, gent., 1745].

BARRY, MICHAEL, 4th s. of Michael, George's Quay, Cork and Eliza McSwiney, b. 23 September 1810; ed. T.C.D. H 1829. G.I., M 1831. H 1834.

BARRY, MICHAEL FRANCIS, 2nd s. of Thomas, Cork, attorney, and Ellen Harding; ed. Queen's College. H 1866.

BARRY, MICHAEL JOSEPH, 1st s. of Michael Joseph, Cork, merchant, and Anne England; b. 26 March 1817; ed. Carlow College. M 1834. G.I., E 1837. E 1839.

BARRY, PATRICK, s. of William, Youghal, Co. Cork, merchant, decd.; under 23; ed. Castleknock; afft. James, attorney, brother. H 1848.

BARRY, PHILIP, 1st s. of James, Carrigleh, Co. Cork, decd. M.T., M 1761. T 1769.

BARRY, REDMOND, 1st s. of James, late of Bath, and Eliza Green; aged 24; ed. T.C.D. L.I. April 1787. Nov. 1792.

BARRY, REDMOND, 3rd s. of Major-General [Henry], Ballyclough, Co. Cork, decd., and Phoebe Drought; b. 8 July 1813; ed. T.C.D. M 1834. L.I., E 1837. M 1838. [Judge of the Supreme Court, Victoria].

BARRY, REDMOND, s. of Robert, Ballinacurra, Co. Cork, merchant; under 19; ed. Bristol; afft. John, brother. E 1849.

BARRY, RICHARD, attorney Exchequer before 1785 r.

BARRY, RICHARD BARNETT, 1st s. of Richard, Lower Glasheen, Cork, and Ellen Barnett; ed. p.t.; formerly a woolen draper. E 1846.

BARRY, ROBERT, s. of Dr. Edward, Dublin; b. Dublin; ed. T.C.D. L.I., T 1750. E 1759 [Senashall of King's Manors. Commissioner of Appeals, K.C.].

BARRY, ROBERT, attorney Exchequer, Dec. 1787, ms.

BARRY, ROBERT, 2nd s. of Rev. Thomas, Rector of Rathclareen, Co. Cork, and Martha Ellen Ryder; b. 20 January 1791; ed. T.C.D. H 1809. M.T., H 1811. T 1819.

BARRY, ROBERT DEEY, s. of Robert, Upper Merrion Street, Dublin, and Mary Deey; over 16; ed. Portora; afft. father. M 1828.

BARRY, SAMUEL, attorney Exchequer, E 1805 r.

BARRY, SWIFT, attorney, T 1733.

BARRY, THOMAS, attorney, T 1776.

Page from E. Keane at al (eds), "King's Inns Admission Papers 1607-1867".

Chapter 16   Family Histories

The genre of historical literature generally described as 'family history' includes several sub-genres of differing value to the genealogical researcher. At the outset it must, of course, be stressed that it is a very optimistic beginner in genealogy that will expect to find his or her direct ancestry recorded in a published work, but what the beginner can hope to find is an account of the history of some dominant branch of the same surname. A general description of some of the varieties of family history, coded to the bibliography which follows, will be helpful to the reader in assessing the value of a particular work. The standard bibliography of this subject is Brian De Breffny's *Bibliography of Irish Family History and Genealogy* (1974).

The 'rara avis' of family histories is that which can lay some claim to being relevant as a genealogical source for any bearer of the surname. Typically, such in-depth treatment is only applicable to a surname of some degree of rarity and/or identified only with a specific region and will have a corresponding level of interest to the general researcher. Beamish (1950), Mellifont (Malenfant) (1980) and Galwey (1963) are Cork-interest examples of this type, identified in the bibliography as type (A).

Another category of family history is that which attempts a detailed genealogical study of a branch or branches of a family. Commonly, this is a prominent landowning or merchant family and the treatment is brought up to the compiler's own time. This sub-genre includes some excellent genealogical studies (e.g. Nagle, Coppinger), but is always elitist in nature, ignoring minor stems of the main branch and ignoring the common bearers of the surname. This type of treatment would include most of the pedigrees printed in reference works such as *Burke's Landed Gentry*. On the positive side, however, it should be said that if a printed pedigree or family history exists for a surname of some rarity in this category, it will always merit close scrutiny (e.g. Conron, Pyne). Identified as (B).

An increasingly common variant of this type are publications by family historians of the results of their research into their own family tree (Leahy (1985), Ronan (1981)). These can be valuable as case studies in research methodology or in emigration patterns and may serve as models of published research, but are unlikely to interface with the researches of the vast majority of bearers of the surname. They may include background information, the value of which will depend on the compiler's experience. Identified as (b).

A third category of family history blends historical narrative with genealogical details. To the naive beginner, this approach will sometimes cause a quickening of the pulse, particularly if Christian names identified in their personal researches are encountered in a 'family history' of substance. However, the pool of Christian names used by Irish families in the past was not large and within each surname there were traditional Christian names with historical associations that recurred regularly across unrelated branches, e.g. among the McCarthys, the names of Florence and Justin. Identified as (C).

Finally, the most general type of family history, usually found in essay form, is the historical treatment on a broad canvas of the documented and historically significant branch(es) of a family. This treatment, accomplished in thumbnail sketches by works such as MacLysaght's, is a record of one's heritage, but is rarely of value in a genealogical search. Typically this treatment of a family ends in the late seventeenth century when the native Irish landowning families were finally dispossessed. D. O'Murchadha's *Family Names of County Cork* (Dublin, 1985; paperback edition, Cork, 1996) is an excellent example of this type, with essay-length sketches on the history of 50 of County Cork's principal families. Identified as (D).

Allman: S. & M. Prentice, *Bear and Forbear: A genealogical study of the Prentice...and related families in GB, Ireland and Australia* [Allmans in County Cork pp. 76-102; Dowdens in County Cork, pp. 103-118], Brisbane, Australia, 1984 (B)

Baldwin: *see* Poole

Barry: Rev. E. Barry, 'Barrymore: Records of the Barrys of County Cork from the earliest times to the present time, with pedigrees', 1902, reprinted from *JCHAS* Vols 5-8, 1899-1902 (B)

Barter: R. ffolliott and M. Leader, 'The Irish Barters' in *IG*, Vol 3, No. 6, 1961 (A)

Beamish: C. T. M. Beamish, *Beamish: A genealogical study of a Family in County Cork and Elsewhere*, London, 1950 (A)

Besnard: T. E. Evans, 'Notes of the Besnard Family', in, *JCHAS*, Vol. 39, 1934. (A)

Burke: B. O'Connell, 'The Rt. Hon. Edmund Burke (1729-1797): a basis for a pedigree' in *JCHAS* Vols 60, 61, 1955-56 (B)

Carew: P. MacCotter, 'The Carews of Cork' in *JCHAS*, Vols 98, 99, 1993-94 (C)

Chinnery: R. ffolliott, 'Chinnery of County Cork' in *IA* Vol. 7 No. 2, 1975 (B)

Clayton: J. P. Rylands, *The Clayton Family of Thelwall, County Chester, afterwards of St Dominick's Abbey, Doneraile and Mallow County Cork*, Liverpool, 1880 (B)

Coghill: *see* Cramer

Cole: R. L. Cole, *The Cole Family of West Carbery*, Belfast, 1943 (B)

Condon: Robt. J. Condon, *Condon Aboos!: the history of an ancient family*, 4th ed, Florida, 1995 (C)

Conron: H. D. Galwey, 'The Conron Family of County Cork' in *IG*, Vol. 3, No. 9, 1964 (B)

Coppinger: W. A. Copinger, *History of the Copingers or Coppingers of County Cork and the Counties of Suffolk and Kent*, Manchester, 1884 (B)

Cotter: J. Coleman, 'Notes on the Cotter Family of Rockforest, County Cork', in *JCHAS*, Vol. 14, 1908; G. De P. Cotter, 'The Cotter Family of Rockforest', in *JCHAS*, Vol. 43, 1938 (B)

Cox: J. H. R. Cox, *Particulars of the Ancestry of Cox of Dunmanway, Bt, County Cork*, London, 1912 (B)

Cramer: B. A. C. Windle, 'A Genealogical Note on the Family of Cramer or Coghill' in *JCHAS*, Vol. 16, 1910 (C)

Crone: B. De Breffny, 'Crone of Cork', in *IA* Vol. 1, No. 2, 1969 (B)

Crowley: J. T. Collins, 'The O'Crowleys of Coill t-Sealbhaigh', in *JCHAS*, Vols 56-58, 1951-53 (D)

Davies: H. E. Jones, 'The Descendants of Very Rev. Rowland Davies, LLD, Dean of Cork', in *IG*, Vol. 3, No. 11, 1966 (B)

Dennehy: 'Family Register of John Dennehy of Fermoy', in, *IG*, Vol. 1, No. 1, 1937 (B)

Denny: Rev. H. L. Denny, Dennys of Cork, in *JCHAS*, Vol. 28, 1922 (C)

Devonsher: R. ffolliott, 'Devonsher of County Cork' in *IA*, Vol. 16, No. 2, 1984 (B)

Dowdens: *see* Allman

Drew: 'The Drews of Mocollop Castle', in *JCHAS*, Vol. 24, 1918 pp 4-6 (B)

Earbery: B. De Breffny, 'Earbery of Ballincollig and Shandangan, County Cork', in *IA*, Vol. 13, No. 2, 1981 (A)

ffolliott: R. ffolliott, 'ffolliott of County Cork', in *IA*, Vol. 17, No. 1, 1985 (B)

Fitzgerald: 'The Fitzgeralds of Glenane, County Cork', in *Journal of the Royal Society of Antiquaries of Ireland*, Vol. 2, 6th s, 1912 (D)

Fleetwood: Sir E. Bewley, 'The Fleetwoods of County Cork' in *Journal of the Royal Society of Antiquaries of Ireland*, 5th s, Vol. 18, 1903 (C)

Fleming: L. T. Fleming, *Fleming and Reeeves of County Cork*, 1971 (B); *see also* Poole

Galwey: Sir Henry Blackall, 'The Galweys of Munster' in *JCHAS*, Vols 71-74, 1966-69 (A); C. J. Bennett, *The Galweys of Lota*, Dublin, 1901 (B)

Green: H. Swanzy & T. Green, *The Family of Green of Youghal, County Cork: being an attempt to trace the descendants of Simon Green, Merchant*, Dublin, 1902 (B)

Gray: R. Clarke & C. Dowman, 'Gray of Cork City and Lehana', in *IA*, Vol. 7 No. 1, 1975 (B)

Harmon: 'The Harmons of Cork', in *IG*, Vol. 3, No. 12, 1967 (B)

Hartland: S. Crowley, 'The Hartland Nursery Family of Mallow and Cork', in *Mallow Field Club Journal*, No. 3, 1985 (C)

Healy: J. T. Collins, 'The Healys of Donoughmore' in *JCHAS* Vol. 48, (D) 1943; Donal Healy, *The Healy Story: heritage of an Irish name*, Macroom, County Cork, 1996 (C)

Herrick: R. ffolliott, 'The Herricks of Cork', in IG Vol. 3, No. 8, 1963 (B)

Hoare: Edward Hoare, *Some account ...of the families of Hore and Hoare*, London, 1883 (B)

Hopper: B. S. Elliott, 'The Hopper Family', in IA, Vol. 16, No. 2, 1982 (A)

Hurley: Rev. P. Hurley, 'Some Account of the Family of O'Hurly' in *JCHAS*, Vols 11, 12, 1905-06 (D)

Jephson: M. D. Jephson, *An Anglo-Irish Miscellany: some records of the Jephsons of Mallow*, Dublin , 1964 (A)

Kingston: A. R. Kingston, 'The Origin of County Cork Kingstons', in *JCHAS*, Vol. 86, 1981 (C)

Lavallin: G. Berkley, 'History of the Lavallins' in *JCHAS*, Vols 30, 31, 1925-26 (C)

Leahy: C. M. Diamond, *The Children of the Settlers* [Descendants of Ml. Leahy of Mitchelstown, Robinson emigrant 1825], Toronto, 1985 (b)

Limrick: Rev. H. L. Denny, 'The Family of Limrick of Schull County Cork' in *JCHAS*, Vol. 13, 1907 (B)

Long: J. T. Collins, 'The Longs of Muskerry and Kinalea', in *JCHAS*, Vol. 51, 1946 (D)

Lyne: G. J. Lyne, 'Dr Dermot Lyne: An Irish Catholic landholder in Cork and Kerry under the Penal Laws', in *JKAHS*, No. 8, 1975 (B)

McAuliffe: D. H. Allen, *The McAuliffes of Clanawley,* Newmarket, County Cork, 1991 (D)

McCarthy: S. T. McCarthy, *The MacCarthys of Munster*, Dundalk, 1922, and, *A MacCarthy Miscellany*, Dundalk, 1928 (C); D. McCarthy, *Historical Pedigree of the Sliocht Feidhlimidh, the MacCarthys of Gleannacroim,*Exeter, 1849 (B); John O'Donovan, 'Pedigree of Mac Carthy of Dunmanway, Chief of Gleann-a-Chroim', in *Annals of the Four Masters*, ed. J. O'Donovan, appendix, pp 2483-2493, Dublin, 1856, reprinted 1990 (B)

Madden: S. Macoboy, 'The Co. Cork Ancestry of the Maddens of Travancore, Melbourne', Australia in *IA*, Vol. 16, No. 1, 1984 (B)

Mansfield: M. Cahill, 'Mansfield — bakers — Mallow, Melbourne, Geelong', in *Mallow Field Club Journal*, No. 12, 1994 (B)

Marmion: Chev. W. F. K. Marmion, *The Marmion Family in Ireland and in General*, 1997 (A)

Meade: J. A. Meade, *The Meades of Meaghstown Castle and Tissaxon, 1300-1766*, and, *The Meades of Innishannon*, Victoria, BC, 1953, 1956; *see also* Poole (C)

Mellefont: A. V. Mellefont, *Malenfant Families: a collection of information about those families who became Malenfaunt, Mellefont, Mellifont and Maliphant*, NSW, 1983, with supplements in 1989 and 1993 (A)

Mitchell: L. R. V. Mitchell & R. ffolliott, 'The Mitchells of Mitchellsfort, County Cork', in *IA*, Vol. 17, No. 2, 1895 (B)

Morgan: *see* Poole

Morris: *see* Poole

Morrogh: F. J. Vaughan, 'The Morroghs of Kilworth, County Cork', in *IA*, Vol. 17, No, 2, 1985 (B)

Mullane: J. T. Collins, 'The Maternal Ancestry of Daniel O'Connell: the O'Mullanes of Brittas and Whitechurch, County Cork', in *JCHAS*, Vol. 54, 1949; Sir H. Blackall, 'The O'Mullanes and Whitechurch', in *JCHAS*, Vol. 58, 1953; B. O.Connell, 'Catherine O'Mullane', in *IG*, Vol. 2, No. 10, 1953 (B)

Murphy: D. O'Murchadha, 'The Uí Mhurchadha or Murphys of Muskerry, County Cork', in *JCHAS*, Vol. 74, 1969 (D)

Nagle: B. O'Connell, 'The Nagles of Annakissy', in *IG*, Vol. 2, No. 11, 1955; 'The Nagles of Mount Nagle', in *IG*, Vol. 2, No. 12, 1955; 'The Nagles of Garnavilla', in *IG* Vol. 3, No. 1, 1956; 'The Nagles of Ballygriffin' in *IG*, Vol. 3, No. 2, 1957 (B)

O'Callaghan: H. W. Gillman, 'The Chieftains of Pobul-I-Callaghan, County Cork, with Historical Pedigree', in *JCHAS*, Vol, 3, 1897 (D)

O'Connell: Lord Dunboyne, O'Connell of Cork in *IG*. Vol 9, No 3, 1996 (B)

O'Donovan: John O'Donovan, 'Pedigree of O'Donovan' in *Annals of the Four Masters*, ed. John O'Donovan, appendix, pp 2430-2483, Dublin 1856, reprinted 1990 (B)

O'Driscoll: John O'Donovan, 'The Genealogy of Corca Laidhe', in *Miscellany of the Celtic Society*, Dublin, 1849 (D)

O'Mahony: Canon John O'Mahony, 'History of the O'Mahony Septs of Kinelmeaky and Ivagha', in *JCHAS*, Vols 12-16, 1906-1910, separately published as an offprint in 1910; *The O'Mahony Journal: Organ of the O'Mahony Records Society*, Vol, 1 -, 1971- (C)

O'Regan: J. T. Collins, 'The O'Regans of Carbery', in *JCHAS*, Vol. 63, 1958 (D)

O'Sullivan: G. J. Lyne, 'The Mac Finin Duibh O'Sullivans of Tuosist and Berehaven', In *Kerry Arch. and Hist. Soc. Journal*, 1976 (B)

O'Hea: J. T. Collins, 'The O'Heas of South-West Cork', in *JCHAS*, Vol. 51, 1946 (D)

Penrose: H. Read, 'The Penroses of Woodhill, Cork' in *JCHAS*, Vol. 85, 1980 (C)

Phair(e): W. H. Welply, 'Colonel Robert Phaire, "Regicide": his ancestry, history and descendants', in *JCHAS*, Vols 29-32, 1924-27 (B)

Poole: R. ffolliott, *The Pooles of Mayfield and other Irish Families* (Poole, Baldwin, Morris, Morgan, Meade, Fleming, Townsend), Dublin, 1958

Power: Rev. J. Coombes, *Notes on the Power Family of Carbery*, 1967 2nd Ed, 1969 (B)

Pratt: J. Pratt, *Pratt Family records: an account of the Pratts of Youghal and Castlemartyr*, 1931 (B)

Punch: T. Punch, 'The Punch Family', in *IG*, Vol. 3, No. 6, 1961, and, 'Pons to Punch', in *IA* Vol. 2, No. 1, 1970 (A)

Puxley: R. O'Dwyer, 'The Puxleys of Dunboy County Cork', in *Irish Family History*, No. 5, 1989 (B)

Pyne: H. F. Morris, 'The Pynes of County Cork', in *IG* vol. 6 No. 6, Vol. 7 ; Nos 1, 2, 1985-87, and, 'The Pynes of County Cork Revisited', in *IG*, Vol 9, No. 4, 1997 (B); F. W. Pyne, *The John Pyne Family in America: being the comprehensive genealogical record of the descendants of John Pyne (1766-1813) of Charleston, SC*, Baltimore USA, 1922 (b)

Quain: F. O'Callaghan, 'The Quains of Mallow', in *Mallow Field Club Journal* No. 8, 1990 (B)

Reeves: *see* Fleming

Rice: M. Dent, 'The Rice Family of Mallow in Australia', in *Mallow Field Club Journal*, No. 14, 1996 (B)

Roche: P. Roche, 'The Roches of Annakisha', in *Mallow Field Club Journal*, No. 14, 1996 (B); W. J. Roche (ed.), *Roche: Mon Dieu est Ma Roche*, Roche Clan publication, 1971 (D)

Rochford: J. Buckley, 'A Cork Branch of the Rochford Family' in *JCHAS*, Vol. 21, 1915 (B)

Rogers: R. ffolliott, 'Rogers of Lota and Ashgrove', in *JCHAS*, Vol 72, 1967 (B)

Ronan: K. R. Cooper, *The Descendants of William and Mary Walsh Ronan of Castlemartyr, County Cork and Middletown, Connecticut 1820-1990*, Baltimore, USA, 1991 (b)

Ronayne: F. W. Knight, 'Notes on the family of Ronayne or Ronan of Counties Cork and Waterford', in *JCHAS*, Vols 22, 23, 1916-17 (B)

Sleigh: A. F. C. Sleigh, *The Sleighs of Derbyshire and Beyond: with pedigree charts*, Havant, Hamps, 1991 (A)

Somerville: Edith & Boyle Somerville, *Records of the Somerville Family of Castlehaven and Drishane form 1174 to 1940*; G. Charles-Edwards, 'The Descent of the Somervilles of Drishane, County Cork', in *IG* Vol. 5, No. 6, 1979 (B)

Spenser: W. H. Welply, 'The Family and Descendants of Edmund Spenser', in *JCHAS*, Vol. 28, 1922 (B)

Spread: B. De Breffny, 'Spread of County Cork', in *IA*, Vol. 2, No. 2 1970 (B)

Stawell: G. D. Stawell (ed.), *A Quantock Family: the Stawells of Cothelstone and their Descendants*, Taunton, (B)

Stout: H. F. Berry, 'The Old Youghal Family of Stout' in *JCHAS*, Vol. 23, 1917 (B)

Swanton: L. M. Swanton, *Swanton Family History Worldwide: from 1242 in England to 1988 in Australia...Ireland...USA*, Baltimore, USA, 1989 (C)

Synan: Rev. J. A. Gaughan, *The Synans of Doneraile*, Dublin, 1971 (C)

Townshend: Richard & Dorothea Townshend, *An Officer of the Long Parliament, being some account of the life and times of Col. Richard Townsend of Castletown (Castletownshend) and a chronicle of his family, [with 13 pedigrees tables]*, London, 1892; *see also* Poole (B)

Trant: S. T. McCarthy, *The Trant Family* and *Supplement to the Trant Family*, Folkestone, no date; J. Hayes, 'The Trants: An enterprising Catholic Family in Eighteenth Century Cork', in *JCHAS*, Vol. 86, 1981 (B)

Uniacke: R. G. Fitzgerald-Uniacke, 'The Uniackes of Youghal', Parts 1-6, (including Uniacke Fitzgerald of Corkbeg), in *JCHAS*, Vol. 3A, 1894 (B)

Waggett: *Some descents of Carson of Shanroe, County Monaghan, attempted by N. D. and T. W. C.*, Dublin, 1879 (B)

Wall: H. Galwey, *The Wall Family in Ireland, 1170-1970*, Naas, 1970 (C)

Waters: E. W. Waters, *The Waters or Walter Family of Cork*, 1939, originally published as 'The Waters Family of County Cork' in *JCHAS*, Vols 31-37, 1926-31 (B)

White: S. Crowley, 'The Whites of Bantry — Family Origins', in *Bantry Historical Journal*, Vol. 2, 1994 (B)

Chapter 17   Miscellaneous Sources

A Source for North County Cork

O'Kief Coshe Mang, Slieve Lougher and Upper Blackwater in Ireland
This 16 volume series was produced in the USA by Dr Albert Eugene Casey. It is known to librarians and researchers as *'O'Kief'*, or *'Coshe Mang'*, or 'them big blue books up there'. It is referred to throughout this book as *O'Kief*. The compilation of sources chiefly refers to the Sliabh Luachra area, but spreads out, in the later volumes particularly, to take in much of Counties Cork and Kerry. Though some believe that Sliabh Luachra is a state of mind rather than a geographical area, it can be roughly designated as the Abbeyfeale-Millstreet-Killarney triangle.

O'Kief in itself is like a library or archive. It is a rag-bag of sources and includes transcripts of parish and civil records, wills, maps, and even whole books. Mixed in with the genealogical material is a collection of the author's anthropological work in which he compares the blood groups, skull measurements etc. of people in the Sliabh Lougher area with those of hundreds of other communities throughout the world.

In typographical design, the books are atrocious. The type of reproduction, while state of the art in the 1950s and 60s when Dr Casey was compiling them, today looks rather crude. The print, for many people, presents problems of legibility. The series is not without typographical errors.

On the positive side, it can be said that *O'Kief* is a remarkable compilation of sources, many of which may not be accessible to someone compiling the same sort of thing nowadays.

Of the first importance are the transcripts of parish registers. The following Catholic parish registers are reproduced: Ballyvourney, Drishane, Dromtarriff, Iveleary (Inchigeela), Kilmeen (Boherbue), and a small portion of Macroom parish (i.e. chronologically, 3 years around 1860s).

O'Kief provides transcripts of a greater number of Church of Ireland records. The following are included: Aghabulloge, Ballyvourney, Buttevant, Carrigamleary, Clondrohid, Clonfert, Doneraile, Donoughmore, Dromtarriff, Inniscarra, Kanturk, Kilshannick, Macroom, Mallow, Mourne Abbey, Rahan. Some of these record compilations are rather brief. Rahan marriage entries for the period 1847-59, for example — a period of thirteen years — comprises only 13 marriages.

Birth, death and marriage records of the Society of Friends, also known as the Quakers, for their three largest communities in County Cork — Cork City, Bandon and Youghal — also appear in *O'Kief*. They date from the mid-seventeenth century, up to the mid-nineteenth century.

In addition to parish registers, the *O'Kief* volumes provide some extracts from the civil records, principally for the baronies of Duhallow and West Muskerry. Duhallow marriage registers are transcribed, from 1845-1900 (1845-1864 being non-Catholic) and births from 1864-1870. West Muskerry marriages from 1864-1900 and births from 1865-1872 are published. Also included in these volumes are transcripts of the will abstacts for counties Cork and Kerry 1858-1900.

Each volume also has a comprehensive index of surnames and Christian names. There are some surnames that obviously lend themselves to searching an index, but if you're looking for someone called John Murphy, you are likely to find about 400 entries in any one of the volumes.

Some people consider the accuracy of the material in *O'Kief* to be somewhat suspect. However, these volumes are probably as accurate as the indexes produced by the various heritage centres throughout the country. At the very least they present an easy finding aid. If one finds what one is looking for, one can always verify the information afterwards in the original. If you have a date, it is relatively easy to ask a parish priest to check the original register, or you can go to the National Library and look up that date in the microfilm records yourself.

The Beara Penisula

Riobard O'Dwyer has published four books on the genealogies of the families who lived on the Beara Peninsula in west Cork. In preparing his work, he studied the parish records, tenant lists, famine statistics and other documentary source material. Most important of all, he sought information from the old people in the area. With their aid he was able to augment and correct the information compiled from the other sources.

In 1976 he published the family trees of the Eyeries parish in a large format book of almost 300 pages titled, *Who Were My Ancestors: Genealogy (Family Trees) of the Eyeries Parish, Castletownbere, Co. Cork, Ireland*. The book slots about 20,000 people from the Eyeries area into their family groups, many extending to five and six generations.

This first book was followed by three similar works: *Allihies (Copper Mines) Parish*; *Bere Island Parish*; *Castletownbere Parish*. At this point the whole Beara Peninsula is covered by Mr O'Dwyer's family tree research. The parishes of Adrigole and Glengarriff & Bonane have not been published but they have been completed in manuscript form.

Mr O'Dwyer's books are available in many libraries. The Eyeries book is now out of print. The other three may be purchased directly from Riobard O'Dwyer (Eyeries Village, Beara, County Cork).

Mr O'Dwyer also accepts research commissions relating to families from the Beara Peninsula.

Hayes's Manuscript Sources

An eleven-volume, published catalogue (edited by R. J. Hayes, 1965) lists National Library manuscripts processed up to 1965. It is also a union catalogue in that it includes manuscript material of Irish interest in other repositories and in private custody in Ireland and overseas (microfilm copies of much of this material is available in the National Library). Entries are arranged by persons, subjects, places and dates. In the case of materials other than those in the National Library the location of the items is given. A three-volume supplement to Hayes, covering the period 1965 -75, has been published, while a card catalogue of material processed in the Library since 1975 is available in the manuscript reading room. It is available in many libraries: in Dublin in the National Library, in Cork in the Cork County Library.

Hayes's *Periodical Sources*

A nine volume published index (edited by R. J. Hayes, 1970) lists all articles, reviews, obituaries and any other substantial features which appeared in a range of Irish periodicals prior to 1970. Entries are arranged by persons, subjects, places and dates. This work has not been updated. For later material you have to look up the relevant periodicals, though for some of these publications, consolidated indexes have been published from time to time. It is available in many libraries: in Dublin in the National Library, in Cork in the Cork County Library.

The Registry of Deeds

The Registry of Deeds was established five years after the passing of the Penal Code and one of its main functions was to ensure the enforcement of legislation which prevented Catholics from buying or taking long leases on land. Up until the 1780s, Catholics could not invest in mortgages or take leases on land for a longer period that 31 years. This situation ensured that Catholics had little to do with the Registry of Deeds during the first 80 years of its existence.

Up to the passing of Gladstone's second land act in 1881, most Irish farmers were tenants-at-will, that is, they had no legal claim to the land and held their farms from year to year on the sufferance of the landlord. Some tenant farmers had leases, but it is not likely that these leases would have been registered. First of all, most leases were short term and those that ran for less than 21 years were exempted from registration. Most leases between landlord and tenant that were registerable were simply retained by the landlord or his agent and were never sent to the Registry of Deeds. There was no point. Registered deeds are made, for the most part, between economic equals or near equals — people who might contemplate taking legal action against one another.

On the other hand, over half a million deeds were registered up to 1832, and at present there are over 3,000,000 deed memorials in the Registry. Obviously, some researchers, those descended from well-to-do ancestors, will strike it lucky. It is worthwhile, therefore, giving a brief outline of how this archive operates.

After the signing of a deed, it was copied, either in its complete form or in the form of a substantial abstract. The copy, known as a 'memorial' was sent off to the Registry of Deeds. There, transcriptions of memorials were written into large, heavy books called 'Abstract and Transcript Books', in date order. The memorial was stored in the vaults in a lead-lined box. If you do intend to carry out your own research, it would be worthwhile studying the appropriate sections of *Irish Genealogy: A Record Finder* or John Grenham's *Tracing Your Irish Ancestors*. A member of the staff of the Registry of Deeds is on hand to show newcomers the ropes.

Orphanages

St Patrick's Orphan Asylum: Annual Reports 1860-1869: annual lists of boys and girls in the orphanage; details of apprenticeships obtained, etc.; annual lists of subscribers, etc.; the source consists of a single volume of collected annual reports in Cork County Library (for a history of the orphanage see: 'St Patrick's Orphanage' in The Fold, November 1959).

'Register of the Boys of St Stephen's Hospital, Cork, from 1st Feb. 1780', ed. M. V. Conlon, in JCHAS, Vol. 62, 1957 pp. 46-55. St Stephen's or the 'Blue-Coat School', was a Protestant charity school. The extracts from the register cover admissions from 1773 to 1802. Names, ages, dates of admission, when and to whom apprenticed. For a history of the school, see Conlon's article in JCHAS, Vol. 48, 1943, pp. 86-7.

Masonic

The Early Years of Harmony Masonic Lodge No. 555 Fermoy, County Cork (1806-1858) by Heron Lepper (1934) — copy in Cork County Library. Two appendices list members of the Lodge and visitors to the Lodge, making it a useful source for army officers, etc., stationed at Fermoy — an important military barracks — during these years.

Minister's Money

'Minister's Money; valuation lists of St Anne's (Shandon) Parish (1793-1853), ed. M. V. Conlon in *JCHAS*, Vol. 47, 1942, pp. 87-111. 'The Valuation Lists for the years 1793, 1804, 1809, 1821, 1832, 1837, 1844 and 1853 were prepared....for the collection of Minister's Money. They show the growth of the parish and serve as a record of the names and addresses of the newly-rated persons. The lists show only the names of the occupants or owners of houses built since the previous valuation'. The lists appear to be transcribed in full. In 1942, these records were in St Anne's, Shandon Church.

Spinning Wheel list

Premium Entitlement lists of the Trustees of the Linen and Hempen Manufacturers of Ireland, 1796' — Better known as the 1796 Spinning Wheel list, it includes 1,061 names from the south-west Cork area, where weaving was an important cottage-industry at that time. A microfiche index was published by All-Ireland Heritage and is available in the National Archives.

Educational Records

Educational records are perhaps more properly considered as biographical than genealogical sources, but they can, in certain circumstances, provide useful information for the family historian. At primary school level, the relevant source is the register of pupils who attended the school. Though the national school system has been in existence since 1831, school registers will rarely date back that far. Among the problems associated with using school records is that of access, as they are not technically public records; another is the matter of establishing the survival and location of the registers of schools that were closed due to population decline and/or amalgamation many years ago. Cork Genealogical Society has been undertaking a survey of national (i.e. primary) school registers for County Cork, which is expected to be completed in 1998.

A handful of County Cork school registers are available in public repositories or have been published in edited form in school histories and are listed below.

School	Parish	Years	Source
Analeentha (boys)	Mourneabbey	1908-1989	*Of School and Scholars: Analeentha*
" (girls)	Mourneabbey	1889-1989	*N.S 1889-1989*
Ballyvongane (boys)	Aghinagh	1866-	*Ballyvongane N.S. 1845-*
" (girls)	Aghinagh	1871-86+	*1995*
Behagh (boys)	Fanlobbus	1854-1992	*Behagh National School 1852-1992*
" (girls)	Fanlobbus	undated	as above
Castlemartyr	Castlemartyr	1889-1989	*Castlemartyr N.S. 1889-1989*
Clontead (boys)	Magourney	1872-1992	*Clontead (Coachford) N.S. 1842-1992*
" (girls)	Magourney	1910-1992	as above
Cork: Christian Brothers College	Cork City	1888-1988	*Christians: The First Hundred Years* Centenary publication (9,200 names)
Cork Model NS	Cork City		Cork Archives Institute & NA
Dromleigh N.S.	Kilmichael	1872-1989	*Memories of Dromleigh 1840-1990*
Kilquane (girls)	Mourneabbey	1871-1889	*Of School and Scholars* see above
Lackareigh N.S.	Kilmichael	1865-1988	*History of Lackareigh N.S. 1865-1988*
Mallow CBS	Mallow	1869-1879	'Students in CBS, Mallow... in *Mallow Field Club Journal*, Nos 3, 4, 1985-86
Terelton N.S.	Kilmichael	1887-1987	*Terelton N.S. 1887-1987*

University education was the preserve of an elite minority until relatively modern times and prior to the establishment of the Queen's Colleges in 1845, the only university in Ireland was Trinity College, Dublin (TCD). *Alumni Dublinenses: a register of the students, graduates, professors, and provosts of Trinity College, in the University of Dublin,* edited by Burtchaell & Sadleir, London, 1924, is a useful genealogical source giving date of matriculation, age, county of birth and father's name and occupation for all students up to 1846. The second edition, published in 1935, has a supplement for the period 1846-60. TCD students in that period were of course predominantly, but not exclusively, Church of Ireland. Registers of the

Alumni of Trinity College, Dublin have also been published at intervals since 1928 and list all graduates of the University believed to be alive at time of publication and all graduates known to have died since the previous issue.

No such convenient sources exist for University College Cork and its predecessors.

Estate Records

While estate records may be the source most likely to take a researcher's family back into the eighteenth century, their scarcity and resistance to location militates against placing them to the forefront of genealogical sources. James S. Donnelly, the historian, has documented in a bibliographic note to his *Land and People in Nineteenth Century Cork* some of the difficulties associated with estate records, the factors that militate against their survival and the locations at that time of a selection of records both in public and private possession relating to County Cork estates.

The process of establishing if records survive for other County Cork estates can at least be initiated by consulting the following sources.

'Survey of Documents in Private Keeping' (first series and second series), in *Analecta Hibernica*, Vol. 15, 1944 and Vol. 20, 1958

A. Eiriksson and C. Ó Gráda, *Estate Records of the Irish Famine*, Dublin, 1995

An inventory of County Cork estate records held by the National Archives and National Library has been produced in a joint project by the Irish Genealogical Society International (IGSI) and the Genealogical Office in Dublin. Further details may be obtained from IGSI, PO Box 16585, St Paul, MN 55116-0585, USA.

Manuscript Sources for the History of Irish Civilisation, already mentioned in this chapter, is a useful finding aid for estate or landlord family records.

Rental Lists

Liam O'Buachalla, Tenant-farmers of the Barrymore Estate 1768 in *JCHAS*, Vol. 51, 1946, pp. 31-40. 'This estate included no less than 107 holdings...and the notices printed here supply the names of townlands, farms, tenant farmers, land agents, middlemen...' The lands were in the parishes of Castlelyons, Carrigtwohill, Caherlag, Middleton, Templerobin, Templeusque.

S. Crowley, 'A Doneraile Rental List', 1823 in *Mallow Field Club Journal*, No. 2, 1984, pp. 162-170.

S. Crowley, 'A Buttevant Rental List' for 1830 in *Mallow Field Club Journal*, No. 7, 1989, pp 88-94.

Contemporary Biographies

Should you be fortunate enough to number among your ancestors somebody who was prominent in business or social circles in early twentieth century Cork, then *Cork and County Cork in the Twentieth Century with Contemporary Biographies*, by R. J. Hodges and W. T. Pike, Brighton, 1911, is worthy of attention. The contemporary biographies section of this large volume comprises of biographical sketches, usually accompanied by a photograph, of over 400 of the city and county's prominent citizens.

Game Certificates

A licence was required in the nineteenth century for killing game and lists of those who had taken out Certificates for Killing Game were published in the press. These lists are naturally dominated by the landed and minor gentry, but also include the gamekeepers on the larger estates.

'County Cork game certificates 1802', R. ffolliott (ed) in *IA*, Vol. 9, No. 1, 1977, pp. 5-15.

'County Cork game Licences, 1821', R. ffolliott (ed) in *IG*, Vol. 8, No. 1, 1990, pp. 79-81.

Game Certificates, 1823 in *Constitution* (newspaper) 10 September 1823.

Records of the old Corporations

In the 1870s, the Cork antiquarian Richard Caulfield published substantial edited extracts from the Council Books of the Corporations of Cork, Youghal and Kinsale. For the family historian researching non-Catholic families that were engaged in trade and commerce in these towns, Caulfield's three volumes contain much of interest — names of those admitted freemen, to whom apprenticed, offices held and roles played in local administration. The indexes to these volumes are minimal, but abstracts were published in *O'Kief* and the indexes to the relevant volumes provide surname access to the thousands of names in Caulfield's records.

The Council Book of the Corporation of the City of Cork from 1609 to 1643, and from 1690 to 1800, edited by Richard Caulfield, Guildford, 1876; abstracted in *O'Kief*, Vol. 7.

The Council Book of the Corporation of Youghal from 1610 to 1659, from 1666 to 1687, and from 1690 to 1800, edited by Richard Caulfield, Guildford, 1878, abstracted in *O'Kief*, Vol. 8.

The Council Book of the Corporation of Kinsale from 1652 to 1800, edited by Richard Caulfield, Guildford, 1879, abstracted in *O'Kief*, Vol. 7.

Minority Religions

While the vast majority of nineteenth century Corkonians professed to be Roman Catholic or Church of Ireland, there were small with locally significant, communities in the Dissenter tradition mainly Methodist, Presbyterians and Quakers. Rarely exceeding one percent of the population, these communities were concentrated in the larger towns and in parts of south-west Cork.

Articles on the records of these religious congregations are included in *Irish Church Records: their history, availabililty and use in family and local history*, edited James G. Ryan, Dublin, 1992. There is also a useful body of literature on the history and development of each of these religions in County Cork, a selection of which is listed below.

Surviving Presbyterian registers for County Cork are now kept at Trinity Presbyterian Church in Cork and include registers for Aghada, Bandon, Clonakilty, Cork, Fermoy, Mallow, and Queenstown congregations. Cork City records date from 1832, Queenstown's from 1847 and those from Bandon for 1842. The registers can be examined by prior arrangement with the minister at the Trinity manse.

Surviving Methodist records for County Cork congregations are likely to be found at either the Cork Manse or the Bandon Manse. The fomer covers the Cork Circuit (e.g. Cork City, Queenstown, Youghal); the latter covers the current West Cork Circuit (i.e., all of West Cork west of Bandon and Kinsale.) PRONI has some transcripts of County Cork Methodists also.

Most original Quaker records are held by the Dublin Friends' Historical Library. However, the Quaker records of birth, marriage and death for the Cork, Bandon and Youghal meetings are transcribed in *O'Kief* Vol. 11.

A History of Congregations in the Presbyterian Church in Ireland 1610-1982, Belfast, 1982

S. O'Saothrai, 'Presbyterianism in Bandon', in, *Bandon Historical Journal*, No. 3, 1987

C. H. Crookshank, *Days of Revival: being the history of Methodism in Ireland*, first published in 3 volumes, 1885, reprinted in 6 volumes, Clonmel, 1994. Supplemented by R. Lee Cole, *History of Methodism in Ireland*, Vol. 4, Belfast, 1960

R. Ó Glaisne, 'History of Methodism in Bandon', in *Bandon Historical Journal* No. 7, 1991

Rev. H. L. F. Bolster, 'Mallow Methodism', in *Mallow Field Club Journal* No. 10, 1992

Olive Goodbody, *Guide to Irish Quaker Records 1664-1860*, Dublin 1957

R. S. Harrison, *Cork City Quakers 1655-1939: a brief history*, Cork, 1991

R . S. Harrison,' The Quakers of Charleville 1661-1742', in *JCHAS*, Vol. 95, 1990

R. S. Harrison, 'The Quakers of Bandon and West Cork 1655-1807', in *Bandon Historical Journal*, No. 10, 1994

Chapter 18   Researching in Cork

Much basic research can be done in Cork without the necessity of travelling to Dublin. The following records are available in Cork in one form or another: the 1901 census returns; civil registration of births, deaths and marriages; valuation and poor law records; tithe applotment books; many parish records; commercial and postal directories; newspapers; graveyard records; electoral lists; family histories; wills and administrations; estate records and many other sources covered in earlier chapters

In this chapter the focus is on the institutions in Cork where research may be carried out, and the people and societies which may be of help, rather than on the records themselves. The contact addresses of all those described below are to be found in the next chapter under the heading 'useful addresses'.

Boole Library, University College Cork

University College Cork's library is called the Boole Library, being named after a mathematician. Its chief function is to facilitate university students but it caters generously for the public. Non-students of the University may be allowed, after being interviewed, to become library members with borrowing facilities, on payment of an annual fee of £25. Alternatively, application may be made for a consultation ticket, the annual fee for which is £10 and, again, is issued, at the discretion of the librarian. A temporary consultation ticket may be issued free of charge. It allows the holder to consult books and documents in the library and is valid for a week or two. It is wise to give two or three days notice if you wish to consult material in the library, especially if you require the use of a microfilm reader which may have to be reserved in advance. Enquiries should be directed to the Boole Library, University College, Cork; phone 021 276871 extension 2199.

From the point of view of the family history enthusiast, the 'special collections' are the most important of the Boole's holdings. The collection includes, the 1901 census, nineteenth century British Parliamentary Papers, and the recently catalogued and very extensive Grehan papers which deal with a north Cork estate. The opening hours for this part of the library are: 9.30 am to 5.00 pm Monday to Friday. Closing time is half-an-hour earlier during the months of July, August and September.

The most interesting item in the 'special collection' section of the library are microfilm reels of the 1901 census covering the counties of Cork, Kerry, Limerick and parts of Waterford.

Cork Archives Institute

The Cork Archives Institute provides an archival service for Cork City and County. It is located at Christ Church, South Main Street, Cork, formerly a church belonging to the Church of Ireland. The service is funded jointly by Cork Corporation, Cork County Council and University College, Cork.

The function of the Archives Institute is to preserve, list and make available to the research community archival records relating to Cork City and County. A reading room is provided where readers, strictly by appointment, may consult lists and original documents.

The quality and range of collections held at the Cork Archives Institute is very extensive and they cover most aspects of Cork's public, political, religious, social and cultural past. They can range in date from the late sixteenth century down to the present day. The Archives Institute is the official repository for the archives of Cork Corporation, Cork County Council and various urban district councils. In addition, it holds records of the poor law unions and various collections of family, estate, business, church and trade union archives. It houses a large quantity of maps, plans and photographs.

Scattered among the disparate collections of the Institute, there is a large amount of genealogical information, much of it available nowhere else. The following is a random list to give some idea of the range and scope of the material. There are details of stallholders in the city markets from 1864, records of people who took out licences to drive hackney cars from 1860, lists of workers employed at Cork Distilleries and other city firms, records of the Earl of Bandon's estate, material relating to the Hare family's estates in Cork and Kerry (where they were known as the Earls of Listowel), baptisms of Unitarian Presbyterians from 1717 to 1799, personal details of girls who were assisted to emigrate from Midleton and Mallow to Canada in the 1840s, a paupers' death register from the 1850s.

Hundreds of boxes of Youghal town records were recently catalogued in a three year programme. This collection, which includes rate books, poll books and other documents relating to the less well-off, will be of particular interest to people with east Cork connections

At the moment the Institute is very understaffed so postal enquiries can be dealt with only if the request is specific — concerns a named individual in an identified set of records.

In the future, the Archives Institute is likely to become a significant Irish repository. There are hopes and plans to transfer its collections to a more suitable building with better storage facilities and more room for public access. In the meantime, it has done invaluable work in preserving records from old city firms, solicitors' offices and other sources, which would otherwise have been destroyed. The Archives Institute undoubtedly holds the answer to many a genealogical riddle, but with much of its materials still packed in the boxes and bags in which they arrived, waiting to be cleaned, sorted and listed, the answers will take time to extract.

Cork Archives Institute is open to te public from Tuesday to Friday from 10.00 am to 1.00 pm and 2.30 pm to 5.00 pm.

Cork City Library

The Cork City Library is situated close to the centre of the city on the Grand Parade, a short walk from the Cork Archives Institute. Apart from adult and children's lending departments, the library has a reference department and a local history department. Entry to both of these departments is free and unrestricted. A friendly and well-informed staff ensure that research is usually relaxed and productive. Though there is a certain amount of duplication in the sources available in the Cork City Library and its county counterpart, their holdings, especially in relation to newspapers and local directories, are basically complementary. The City Library has full collections of important journals such as the *Irish Ancestor* (1969-1986), *the Irish Genealogist* (1937-), *Analecta Hibernica* and the *Journal of the Cork Historical and Archaeological Society* (1892-). A variety of Burke's Peerage publications — including the classic 1912 edition of Burke's *Irish Landed Gentry* — may be consulted in the reference department. The often mentioned *O'Kief Coshe Mang Slieve Lougher and Upper Blackwater in Ireland*, by A. E. Casey is also available.

The library has Griffith's *Valuation* for County Cork in printed volumes and the valuation for the rest of Ireland on microfiche. Another useful local source is Rosemary ffolliott's biographical notices from Cork and Kerry newspapers 1756-1827. It is on microfiche and some parts are difficult to read.

Cork County Library

Like the City Library, researching at the Cork County Library is free and informal. It is located near the County Hall at the western side of the city. Excellent assistance is provided by the staff when required. Many important sources are accessible including postal directories, Griffith's *Valuation* in book form — and the very useful All-Ireland Heritage Index to it — the tithe applotment books for Cork on microfilm, long runs of a representative selection of Cork newspapers commencing around 1820, including a full run of *The Cork Examiner*, the first issue of which was published in 1841. There is a high probability that by the time this book is published, the library will also have a microfilm copy of the 1901 census. As in the City Library, A. E. Casey's *O'Kief Coshe Mang Slieve Lougher and Upper Blackwater in Ireland*, with its very many genealogically relevant transcriptions, is also available.

Cork Court House

The Probate Act of 1857 transferred testamentary jurisdiction from the Church of Ireland to a new court of probate. A Principal Registry was established in Dublin and eleven District Registries were set up to cater for the rest of the country. One such District Probate Registry Office is housed in the Court House, Washington Street, Cork. The office is still busily exercising its statutory functions. It has a small archive which is open to the public on payment of a fee of £1.00. Business hours are from 10.00 am to 4.00 pm, weekdays only.

The research area is in a basement room which is also used to store old manual typewriters, stationery and a photocopying machine. The archive consists of a set of yearly calendars to wills and administrations, commencing with the year 1858 and ending with the year 1957. Later indexes may be consulted in the offices on the ground floor in which the staff carry out their duties.

Abstracts of all administrations granted and of all wills probated since 1858, both in the Principal Registry in Dublin and in the several District Registries, are to be found in the year books. These abstracts are fairly detailed. They give the name, address and marital status of the deceased; the dates of death and probate; the names and addresses of the executors; and also the value of the assets of the deceased.

If you locate a Cork will abstract that you are interested in, you can write to the National Archives for a full copy of the will. Cork is one of the few counties whose wills did not go up in smoke in the Four Courts fire in 1922. The National Archives has will books for Cork from 1858 to 1932. For some reason the will books for the period 1933 to 1952 are in the basement research room in the Cork Court House. Perhaps someone forgot to send them to Dublin?

Very few people seem to come to this district probate office to do research, so you are likely to have the place to yourself.

Cork Family History Centre

The Church of Jesus Christ of Latter-day Saints (the Mormons) founded the Family History Library in 1894. It has become the largest library of its kind in the world. The Genealogical Society of Utah started filming Irish Records in 1948 and has continued with the work on and off since then. At the moment, the Irish collection comprises some 10,000 rolls of microfilm.

In 1964 a system of family history centres was established to give more people access to the library's resources. There are three Mormon family history centres in Ireland: one each in Dublin, Belfast and Cork.

The Library in Salt Lake City and the family history centres are open to the public. The records and resources may be used without charge. If your local centre does not have in stock the particular record you require, there is a rental fee charged to cover the cost of shipping the film, but this is very minimal.

Initially, each centre is given some basic records and essential equipment. The Cork centre, situated in a room behind the Mormon church, has five microfilm/microfiche readers. Its records include two items of standard issue. The first is the Family History Library Catalogue, which lists and describes the records, books, microfilms and microfiche in the Family History Library. It does not contain the actual records, only a description of them. The second item, the International Genealogical Index (IGI), is a world-wide index of more than 147 million names of deceased persons. Individuals are listed alphabetically, a date and the source of the information is given with each entry. They are listed in county-wide, country-wide and world-wide indexes. They are not joined in family groups or pedigrees. There are currently 1,109, 492 entries on the IGI for Ireland. The IGI is revised every four years. The Cork centre also possesses microfilms of the General Register Office indexes to births, deaths and marriages.

A researcher may order anything on the Family History Library Catalogue by paying a fee and having the item shipped to the local centre. If you wish to keep the film at the centre for one month, it costs IR£2.55, retaining it for three months costs IR£3.65, and it costs IR£4.40 to have the film kept permanently at the centre. It takes from six to eight weeks for a film to arrive.

The Mormons believe that their deceased ancestors may be baptised and become posthumous members of the Church of Jesus Christ of Latter-day Saints. This is why they are so interested in genealogy. The research facilities are provided for the use of their own members. They allow non-members to use them as a courtesy. No attempt is made by the Mormons to convert researchers or to influence their religious views in any way. It is expressly forbidden for members of the Mormon Church to broach the subject of religion in their research room.

Cork Genealogical Society

Cork Genealogical Society was founded in March 1994. Though family history is among the most popular hobbies in the world, Ireland has very few local family history societies to cater for enthusiasts. The Cork Society remains the only local family history society in Munster which holds regular meetings.

Meetings are held on the second Tuesday of each month at Moore's Hotel, Morrisons Island, Cork City — except during the months of June, July and August. The usual format is for a speaker to give a talk on some aspect of family history — after the formalities of the meeting — followed by questions and answers, and finally by an informal chat among members. Workshops and visits to local research facilities are also organised.

The annual programme of the society is drawn up at the AGM in March, and displayed in libraries throughout the city and county. Non-members may attend meetings if they find a particular lecture of interest, for an entry fee of £2.00. The annual subscription is £10.00. The society tries to foster an interest in family history, provides a regular discussion forum, and gives guidance to those doing family history research.

There has been considerable interest in the society from abroad, but at present due to lack of resources, very little assistance can be given to researchers who write in looking for help. Such requests are usually read out at meetings and individual members may take it upon themselves to make a response. Many people from abroad have become members of the Society more as a gesture of solidarity and support, rather than for any expectation of services. Occasionally, foreign members who are visiting Cork City turn up at meetings. The Society produces a quarterly newsletter and all members' queries are published therein.

Irish Genealogical Project Centres

The Irish Genealogical Project (IGP) is an all-Ireland effort to index and computerise Irish records of genealogical importance, particularly: the 1901 census, church registers, Griffith's *Valuation*, the tithe applotment books and gravestone inscriptions. The initiative is county-based and many counties have made substantial progress. Cork lags behind due mainly to a dispute that arose between an indexing group in Bandon, County Cork, and the Catholic Church authorities in Cork in November 1989. The situation was resolved to some extent in 1994 and work has resumed in the diocese of Cork. Cork Ancestral Research, the current indexing project in the diocese of Cork is currently engaged in indexing and computerising records for the deanery of Cork (the greater Cork City region). It is not anticipated that a research service will be available from Cork Ancestral Research before 1999. However, the records for the dioceses of Cork and Ross are nowhere near completion. In contrast, the parish registers for the diocese of Cloyne have been indexed and computerised and an IGP research service is available at Mallow Heritage Centre, Bank Place, Mallow.

Professional Genealogists

Tom O'Leary is a professional genealogist, and Munster's only member of the Association of Professional Genealogists in Ireland. He provides a number of useful services to family history enthusiasts. Written assessments of genealogical information are available at a cost of £10/US$20/Can$25. He also provides a consultancy service at his office in Clonakilty. The current rate is £15 for around 30 minutes. This service must be booked in advance and is available Monday to Friday during the months of May and September. He also accepts family history research commissions.

Superintendent Registrars' Offices

The Superintendent Registrars' offices in Cork City, Mallow and Skibbereen have already been comprehensively dealt with in Chapter 5.

Chapter 19   Researching in Dublin

The most important places for doing genealogical research in Dublin are the General Register Office, the National Archives, the National Library of Ireland, the Representative Church Body Library (RCB), and the Valuation Office. Those with an optimistic outlook may also wish to visit the Registry of Deeds. The Genealogical Office is also worth knowing about, though most will find little there to further their researches.

The prospect of entering one of these buildings for the first time can be intimidating. You walk into the National Archives, there is an oppressive, studious atmosphere. People sitting at large tables look up briefly from the scrutiny of files and documents. You take a place at one of the tables. You see people examining indexes, filling up order forms, getting large boxes of documents brought to them by members of the staff. You've come along in the hope of being allowed to rummage through boxes like those, for information about your ancestors, but you don't know the ropes, you slink out.

This chapter aims to briefly introduce the reader to the procedures in the archives listed above; to give enough information to enable the first-timer to make a start. Once the initial foray into any archive is successful to some degree, a working knowledge is rapidly acquired.

The address, phone, fax and e-mail numbers and the opening hours of the archives, for convenience, may be found in Chapter 20, 'Useful Information'.

General Register Office

Full details have already been given in Chapter 5, 'Civil Registration', on the procedures involved in doing research at the General Register Office.

National Archives

It is more difficult for a researcher to cope with a record repository than with a library. In its physical appearance, one book is very much like another. Also, a book normally deals with a particular person, place or subject. It is easy to define the scope of a book and to put it into a category. Books, therefore, can be arranged on shelves and readers can access them easily by means of one or more indexes.

Records are the papers generated over a long period by individuals and organisations in their day to day affairs. Their content is less easy to define. Physically, they vary enormously. They may have to be placed in boxes or files or tied in bundles. Some may be old and require delicate handling. Their physical appearance rather than their subject matter often determines where and how they are stored. The very nature of records, therefore, means that they must be kept in special storage areas to which members of the public do not have access. The only area open to the public at the National Archives is the Reading Room.

Since no original records are kept in the Reading Room a researcher must have some knowledge of what's in storage. There is no comprehensive guide to the records in the National Archives and most of the short guides are both out of print and out of date. It is difficult to keep up with what is available as new material is being acquired all the time. Photocopies of the *Short Guide to the Public Record Office of Ireland* are on sale at the National Archives. Brief descriptions of records obtained from private sources may be found in *Manuscript Sources for the History of Irish Civilisation*. Margaret Dickson Falley's *Irish and Scotch-Irish Ancestral Research* gives a good account of records in the National Archives that could be of interest to the family history enthusiast. Comprehensive, modern articles on record classes and search topics may be found in each issue of *Irish Archives*.

Only when you have become somewhat familiar with the various kinds of records in storage should you go along to the Reading Room. Having acquired a reader's ticket — which has to be renewed each year — you may enter the Reading Room. First, find a vacant place at one of the tables. You may deposit your notebooks, pencils, etc. there to reserve it while you go to the card indexes or typescript indexes and finding aids which are on open access. These searching aids will enable you to find the sections of the records that deal with the townland, parish, estate, barony, district electoral division, poor law union or county that you are interested in. All records have their own call numbers. When you have selected the records that you wish to inspect, you take an call slip from the counter and fill in your name, reader no., the call number of the documents and your table number. Give the docket to the staff at the counter, return to your table and wait for one of the staff to bring you what you are looking for. If you have any problems, there is a helpful staff on hand to give you assistance.

Some of the collections of the National Archives are available on the World Wide Web, such as the transportation records of convicts sent from Ireland to Australia between 1788 and 1868. This material is searchable.

National Library of Ireland

The National Library of Ireland is situated in Kildare Street, near Dáil Éireann and the Genealogical Office. A temporary, non-renewable ticket allowing limited access to the collections may be granted on production of some form of identification. A passport, driving licence or similar document will suffice for this purpose. If you wish to be issued with a full reader's ticket for the Library, you are required to bring two passport size photographs with you.

The Library is about to introduce a Genealogical Advisory Service in a room off the main entrance hall. This will provide basic information on how to go about family history research. It will also direct people to the genealogically relevant material in the Library. First-time researchers availing of this service should feel more confident when they make their initial foray into the main Reading Room and the Microfilm Reading Room.

If you wish to do research in the Manuscript Room, which is not located in the Library complex but above the Genealogical Office a short distance away, you must undergo an interview and additional photographs are required for that ticket.

There is no charge for the tickets nor is there any entry charge to the Library.

It is forbidden to bring a bag, jacket or overcoat into the reading room. If you have any of these items with you, an attendant will place them in a locker, give you the key to it, and return your property when you are leaving. Again, there is no charge for this service. You are required to sign a register at the service counter each day as you enter the reading room. If you use the manuscript reading room you must also sign the register there.

So, finally, you find yourself in the magnificent, domed, reading room of the National Library of Ireland. The book-shelves are against the circular walls, leaving the entire floor space free to accommodate tables and chairs for researchers. At the end of the room opposite the service desk, a door leads to a microfilm reader room. The first thing to do is to get a table or a microfilm reader for yourself by placing your biros, folder, loose pages or other small items of property on top of it. Getting used to the place is made much easier if you know a little about the Library's genealogically-relevant material. Then you can get a book or microfilm, sit down and settle in.

The microfilms of Catholic parish registers are the National Library's most frequently requested resource. Generally, these microfilms may be freely consulted. In the case of parishes in the dioceses of Cloyne, Kerry and Limerick, a letter of authorisation from the bishop must be produced before examining the microfilms. A catalogue of parish registers is available at the service counter. You find the parish you are interested in and transcribe its call number onto a call slip. You fill in other details on the call slip, including your microfilm reader number and hand it to one of the librarians on duty. You then return to your microfilm reader. You can expect a member of the staff to bring whatever you have ordered to your table within fifteen minutes. You can fill out up to three call slips at a time.

Apart from the registers, the library has a large collection of printed books, newspapers, maps, photographs and manuscripts, all of which are accessed in the same way: find the item you want in a catalogue, fill in a call slip and return to your table and wait.

Representative Church Body Library (RCB)

The Representative Church Body Library (RCB) is a little difficult to find. It is situated in Braemor Park, Churchtown in the southern suburbs of Dublin. It takes about 30 minutes to get there by car from the city centre. The number 14 bus from D'Olier to Braemor Park takes a little over half an hour. The bus stop is less than five minutes walk from the Library: ask the driver for directions to Mount Carmel hospital which is on Braemor Park.

The Library is the Church of Ireland's principal reference library and archives and manuscripts repository. It is situated in the grounds of the Church of Ireland Theological College. Parts of its genealogically relevant collections, though, are also relevant to other denominations.

The largest collection of Church of Ireland parish registers is to be found in the RCB Library. An up-to-date, typed list of these holdings is available from the Library for £2.00 plus £0.50 postage and packing.

Miscellaneous papers were deposited with some parish records: documents such as wills, deeds, maps, vestry records including registers of vestrymen, account books and preachers' books.

The records of educational bodies, individual schools, charitable organisations and missionary societies are other possible sources of genealogical information to be found in the Library.

Research papers of Irish clergy are also housed in the Library. Among the most promising from the point of view of the family history researcher are W. H. Welply's collection which consists of pedigree notebooks and files of genealogical research notes on Munster, particularly Cork, families from the seventeenth to the twentieth centuries.

The public has a right of access to pre-disestablishment Church of Ireland parish registers, however, no such right exists as far as other materials in the Library are concerned. Permission may be granted, free of charge, to those wishing to read in the Library during the normal opening hours. Though application in advance is not required it would be prudent to phone before calling, especially if your research requires the use of a microfilm reader or access to original documents. Photocopying will be undertaken at the discretion of the librarian and archivist.

Valuation Office

The Valuation Office recently moved from its premises at 6 Ely Place, to the Irish Life Building, Middle Abbey Street, Dublin 1. It houses the 'cancelled books' and the valuation maps referred to in Chapter 7, 'Griffith's *Valuation*'.

People engaged in genealogical research are charged at the rate of Ir£12.00 per hour or £2.00 per book examined. The staff in the front office usually try to give the visitor some explanation of the records he/she has come to inspect. The visitor is then conducted to the search room, where more help is available if required.

No appointment is necessary to visit the Office and the number of callers does not result in overcrowding.

Registry of Deeds

The Registry of Deeds was established in 1708 and today, 290 years later, it still carries out its function of registering deeds concerning land transactions. What is even more impressive is the fact that its entire archive has survived intact and perfectly preserved. The Registry of Deeds is open to the public, and for the very modest fee of £2.00 you can spend the entire day leafing through its massive manuscript volumes of indexes and deed transcripts. This great collection is housed in a neo-classical building with stone stairs, gloomy rooms and labyrinthine passages — just the place where genealogical discoveries seem tantalisingly close.

The bad news, however, is that the great bulk of the material in this archive concerns only a tiny minority of the Irish people who lived during the last three centuries. For most researchers, time spent in the Registry of Deeds is time wasted.

There are two indexes to the material in the Registry of Deeds: a 'Names Index' and a 'Lands Index'. The 'Names Index' lists the grantors in alphabetical order in volumes covering periods which vary from two to twenty-one years. The 'Lands Index' is arranged by county. Each county is subdivided into baronies. Townlands which are the subject of entries are listed under the barony in which they are situated. Like the 'Names Index', the 'Lands Index' does not cover the entire period as a single unit. It is a series of indexes in which consecutive periods are covered. The indexes lead to the transcripts in the 'Abstract and Transcript Books' which you can access immediately and personally, and to the memorials. If you want to see a memorial, an inspection fee of £1.00 is payable and the memorial is usually made available the following day. A copy of a memorial costs £4.00. Some of the older memorials may have signatures and seals attached

Rosemary ffolliott and other commentators have suggested that the Registry of Deeds is a difficult source for the amateur genealogist to tackle and advise the employment of a professional researcher.

Genealogical Office

The Genealogical Office is situated centrally in Kildare Street, a short distance from the National Library and Trinity College. The entrance leads into the Heraldic Museum which has many items such as flags and seals on display. For most people, the only thing available at the Genealogical Office relevant to family history research is advice. Members of the Association of Professional Genealogists in Ireland have been running a consultancy service there for many years. However, this is to be terminated shortly as the National Library is introducing its own scheme.

Most of the official records of the Genealogical Office relate to heraldry: grants of arms, confirmation of arms, registration of pedigrees. The bulk of such records relate to the Anglo-Irish and most date from the nineteenth century. Many other records were deposited in the office from time to time but are too much of a rag-bag to list here. A full account of the records of the Office may be found in John Grenham's *Tracing Your Irish Ancestors*, pp 67-90.

Chapter 20   Useful Information

Useful Addresses: Cork

Boole Library,
University College, Cork;
Phone: 021 276871 extension 2199.

Cork Archives Institute,
South Main Street, Cork;
Phone: 021 277809;   Fax: 021 274668.

Cork City Library,
Grand Parade, Cork;   Phone: 021 277110.

Cork County Library,
Farranlea Road, Cork; Phone: 021 546499.

Cork Courthouse,
Probate Registry, Washington Street, Cork;
Phone: 021 271223.

Cork Family History Centre,
Sarsfield Road, Wilton, Cork;
Phone: 021 874858.

Cork Genealogical Society,
c/o 4 Evergreen Villas,
Evergreen Road, Cork City.

Mallow Heritage Centre (IGP),
27-28 Bank Place,
Mallow, County Cork;   Phone: 022 21778

Professional Genealogist
Thomas O'Leary,
7 Wolfe Tone Street,
Clonakilty, County Cork;
Phone: 023 34448.   e-mail: duchas@iol.ie

Superintendent Registrar's Office
18 Liberty Street, Cork City;
phone: 021 275126.

Superintendent Registrar's Office
County Council Offices, Annabella,
Mallow;   Phone: 022 21123.

Superintendent Registrar's Office
The Courthouse, Skibbereen;
Phone: 028 21299.

Cork Ancestral Research Ltd,
c/o Cork County Library,
Farranlea Road, Cork; Phone: 021 546499.

The Main Irish Archives:
Addresses & Opening Times
More detailed information on these archives is to be found in chapter 19.

Genealogical Office,
2 Kildare Street,
Dublin 2;
Phone: (01) 6030200;   Fax: (01) 6766690

OPENING HOURS:
MONDAY TO FRIDAY, 10.00 AM TO 12.45 PM,
AND 2.00 PM TO 4.30 PM.

General Register Office,
Joyce House,
8-11 Lombard Street East,
Dublin 2;
Phone: (01) 6711000;   Fax: (01) 6711243

OPENING HOURS:
MONDAY TO FRIDAY, 9.30 AM TO 12.30 PM

AND 2.15 PM TO 4.30 PM.

National Archives,
Bishop Street, Dublin 8;
Phone: 014072300;   Fax: 01 4072333.

OPENING HOURS:
MONDAY TO FRIDAY, 10.00 AM TO 5.00 PM.

National Library of Ireland,
Kildare Street, Dublin 2;
Phone: (01) 6030200;   Fax: (01) 6766690

OPENING HOURS:
MONDAY: 10.00 AM TO 9.00 PM;
TUES & WED: 2.00 PM TO 9.00 PM;
THURS & FRI: 10.00 AM TO 5.00 PM;
SATURDAY: 10.00 AM TO 1.00 PM

114   *A Guide to Tracing your Cork Ancestors*

Registry of Deeds,
Henrietta Street, Dublin 1;
Phone: (01) 8732233

Opening Hours:
Monday to Friday, 10.00 am to 4.30 pm.

Representative Church Body Library (RCB),
Braemor Park,
Churchtown, Dublin 14;
Phone: (01) 4923979; Fax: (01) 4924770

OPENING HOURS:
MONDAY TO FRIDAY, 9.30 AM TO 1.00 PM,
AND 1.45 PM TO 5.00 PM.

Valuation Office,
Irish Life Complex,
Middle Abbey Street, Dublin 1;
Phone: (01) 8171000; Fax: (01)

OPENING HOURS:
9.30 AM TO 12.30 PM; AND 2.00 PM TO 4.30 PM.

Useful Genealogical Publications

The following publications are widely available and will give
the reader a better understanding of Irish genealogy.

The Irish Roots Guide
Tony McCarthy

Tracing Irish Ancestors
Máire MacConghail and
Paul Gorry

Tracing Your Irish Ancestors
John Grenham

Irish and Scotch Irish Ancestral Research
Margaret Dickson Falley

Irish Church Records
James G. Ryan (Editor)

Irish Genealogy: A Record Finder
Donal Begley (Editor)

Irish Records: Sources for Family and Local History
James G. Ryan

Irish Roots Magazine,
(quarterly publication)
Belgrave Publications,
Belgrave Avenue, Cork.

Bibliography
The Poor Law Records of County Cork, Cork Archives Institute, 1995,

S. Helferty & R. Refauseé (eds): *Directory of Irish Archives*, second edition, Dublin, 1993.

Cork Interest
James S. Donnelly: *The Land and People in Nineteenth Century Cork: the rural economy and the land question*, (with extensive bibliography), London, 1975, paperback, 1987

Evelyn Bolster: *A History of the Diocese of Cork* (4 vols), Vol. 1, Shannon, 1972, vols 2-4, Cork 1982-93

Colman O'Mahony: *In the Shadows: life in Cork 1750-1930*, Cork, 1997

Dictionary of townlands and district electoral division in the county of Cork; ed. E. Marnane. Cork, 1985.

Grove-White, James, *Historical and topographical notes* (on North Cork) 4 vols. Cork, 1905-1918.

O'Donoghue, B. *Parish histories and place names of West Cork.* Cork, 1986.

Cork: history and society; ed. by P. O'Flanagan and C. Buttimer. Cork, 1993.

William Maziere Brady: *Clerical and Parochial records of Cork, Cloyne and Ross,* (3 vols) Dublin, 1863-64

J. H. Cole: *Church and Parish Records of the United Dioceses of Cork, Cloyne and Ross,* Cork, 1903

Ian d'Alton: *Protestant Society and Politics in Cork 1812-1844,* Cork, 1980

D. D. C. P. Mould: *Discovering Cork,* Dingle, Co. Kerry, 1991

Rev. W. Holland: *History of West Cork and the Diocese of Ross,* Skibbereen, 1949

General Interest

Lewis, Samuel. *Topographical dictionary of Ireland.* 2 vols. (London, 1837) and later eds.

MacLysaght, E. *Irish families: their names, arms and origins.* Dublin, 1957; 4th ed. 1985.
More Irish families. Dublin, 1970. 2nd ed., 1982, incorporating *'Supplement to Irish families'* (1964).

de Bhulbh, S. *Sloinnte na h.Eireann/Irish Surnames.* Limerick,1997.

Hickey, D.J. and Doherty, J.E., *A dictionary of Irish History since 1800.* Dublin, 1980.

Index

A

Abbeymahon, 25, 60, 65
Abbeystrewry, 25, 60
Abbreviations, 8
Administrations, 103
Administrative divisions, 21
Adrigole, 94
Aghabulloge, 25, 29, 60, 93
Aghacross, 25, 79
Aghada, 25, 27, 29, 36, 56, 60, 100
Aghadown, 25, 28, 56, 61
Aghern, 25, 26
Aghinagh, 25, 56, 77, 97
Aglish, 25, 61
Aglishdrinagh, 25
Ahern, 61
Allihies, 94
All-Ireland Heritage Inc, 50
Allman, 88
Anakissy, 26, 29, 36, 56, 90
Ardagh, 25, 61
Ardfield, 25, 29, 56, 61
Ardnageehy, 25, 61
Ardskeagh, 25
Army, 83
Assizes, 71
Athnowen, 25, 28, 61
Australia, 15, 19

B

Baldwin, 88
Ballinaboy, 25, 61
Ballinadee, 25, 61
Ballinamona, 56
Ballincollig, 26, 27, 28, 56, 77, 83, 89
Ballindangan, 56, 57
Ballinhassig, 25, 27, 36, 56
Ballintemple, 25
Ballyagran, 27
Ballyclogh, 26, 27, 28, 56, 77
Ballycurrany, 26, 77
Ballydeloher, 26
Ballydeloughy, 26
Ballydesmond, 16
Ballyfeard, 26, 61
Ballyfoyle, 26

Ballygran, 56
Ballygriffin', 90
Ballyhay, 25, 26, 27, 28, 29, 56, 61
Ballyhooly, 26, 28, 40, 61
Ballymacoda, 26, 27, 28, 56
Ballymartle, 26, 56, 61, 78
Ballymodan, 26, 39, 61, 77
Ballymoney, 26, 52, 61
Ballynoe, 26, 61, 77
Ballyoughtera, 26
Ballyspillane, 26
Ballyvongane, 97
Ballyvourney, 26, 39, 52, 53, 56, 61, 77, 93
Bandon, 17, 26, 28, 39, 45, 56, 68, 69, 77,
  78, 82, 93, 100, 102, 105
Banns, 65
Banteer, 56
Bantry, 45, 56, 77
baptisms, 55, 59
Barnahely, 26
Barony, 22
Barry, 88
Barrymore, 28, 88, 98
Barryroe, 56
Barter, 88
Beamish, 87, 88
Beara Historical Society, 77
Beara peninsula, 17, 73
Behagh, 97
Bere Island, 77, 94
Berehaven, 28, 61, 91
Besnard, 88
Biographies, 98
Births (civil) 41
Blackrock, 56
Blackwater Valley, 16
Blarney, 27, 36, 56
Blessing, Patk.J., 16
Bohillane, 26, 61
Bonane, 56, 94
Boole Library (UCC), 101, 113
Boston, 16
Boston Pilot, 17
Bregoge, 26
Bridgetown, 26, 61

Schools, 97, 110
Schull/Skull, 28, 36, 45, 58, 61, 64, 90
Seamen, 84
Shandrum, 36, 58, 64
Shipping, 71
Skibbereen, 25, 27, 36, 42, 45, 58, 73, 106, 113, 115
Skull *See* Schull
Sleigh, 92
Somerville, 92
Sosa Stradonitz, 11
Spenser, 92
Spinning Wheel list, 96
Spread, 92
St Anne Shandon, 24
St Anne's (Shandon), 96
St Anne's Shandon, 29, 62
St Finbar, 24, 29, 54, 58, 62, 75, 77
St Luke's, 62
St Mary & St Anne, 58
St Mary Shandon, 40
St Mary's, 27, 29, 58, 62, 79
St Michael's, 29, 62
St Nathlash, 29, 52
St Nicholas, 24, 29, 62
St Patrick's, 58
St Paul's, 27, 29, 62
St Peter and Paul's, 58
St Peter's, 27, 36, 62, 77, 79
Stawell, 92
Stout, 92
Subulter, 36, 64
Summerhill, 79
Swanton, 92
Synan, 92

T

Templebodan, 36, 64
Templebreedy, 36
Templebryan, 36, 65
Templemartin, 36, 58, 65
Templemichael, 36, 65
Templemolaga, 36
Templenacarriga, 36, 65
Templeomalus, 36, 65
Templequinlan, 36, 65
Templeroan, 36, 65
Templerobin, 36, 98
Templetrine, 36, 65
Templeusque, 36, 98

Tenure books, 48
Terelton, 97
Timoleague, 25, 27, 28, 29, 36, 58, 65, 80
Tisaxon, 36, 80
Titeskin, 36, 80
Tithe applotment, 49, 52, 105
Tithe Defaulters, 52
Tithe war, 51
Tithes, 21, 51
Townland, 21-24
Townland Index, 37, 49
Townshend, 92
Trabolgan, 36
Tracton, 26, 28, 29, 36, 57, 58, 65
Trade union, 102
Trant, 92
Trinity College, Dublin, 97
Troy, Canon B., 25, 39, 55
Tullagh, 65
Tullilease/ Tullylease, 36, 65, 80

U
Uniacke, 92
Universities, 97

V
Valuation Maps, 49
Valuation Office, 110, 114
Voters, 81

W
Waggett, 92
Wall, 92
Wallstown, 36, 52, 65
Watergrasshill, 25, 28, 58
Waterloo Directory, 73
Waters, 92
Welply Collection, 110
White, 92
Whitechurch, 36, 65, 90
Wills, 21, 84, 93, 101, 103, 110
Workhouse, 23, 47

Y
Youghal, 26, 36, 42, 45, 58, 65, 68, 80, 81, 82, 89, 91, 92, 93, 99, 100, 102